THE MIRACLE OF LIFE

JAN DE VRIES was born in 1937 in Holland and grew up during the difficult war years in occupied territory. Although he graduated in pharmacy, he soon turned to alternative medicine. His most influential teacher was Dr Alfred Vogel in Switzerland, and they have worked together closely for 35 years.

In 1970 he and his family moved to Scotland and settled on the west coast in Troon, where he set up a residential clinic called Mokoia. He also has clinics in Newcastle, Edinburgh and London. Since 1990 he has been involved in Klein Vink in Arcen, Holland, doing research into the efficacy of herbal medicine for the European Commission.

He lectures throughout the world and is a regular broadcaster on BBC radio.

Books available by the same author

By Appointment Only series:

Stress and Nervous Disorders (3rd impression)
Multiple Sclerosis (4th impression)
Traditional Home and Herbal Remedies (5th impression)
Arthritis, Rheumatism and Psoriasis (5th impression)
Neck and Back Problems (4th impression)
Migraine and Epilepsy (3rd impression)
Cancer and Leukemia (2nd impression)
Viruses, Allergies and the Immune System (4th impression)
Realistic Weight Control (2nd impression)
Who's Next?
Heart and Blood Circulatory Problems
Asthma and Bronchitis
Life Without Arthritis — The Maori Way
Skin Diseases

Nature's Gift series:

Body Energy (2nd impression)
Water — Healer or Poison?
Food

Well Woman series:
Menstrual and Pre-menstrual Tension

THE MIRACLE OF LIFE

JAN DE VRIES

MAINSTREAM
PUBLISHING

This edition 1992
First published Great Britain 1987 by
MAINSTREAM PUBLISHING COMPANY (EDINBURGH) LTD
7 Albany Street
Edinburgh EH1 3UG

Reprinted 1988, 1989, 1999

ISBN 1 85158 469 2

A catalogue record for this book is available from the British Library

Printed and bound in Great Britain by J.W. ArrowsmithLtd, Bristol

Contents

To my four "Miracles"

Fiona   *Janyn*   *Tertia*   *Mhairi*

For those who believe in God,
No explanation is necessary;
For those who do not believe in God
No explanation is possible.

John La Farge.

Introduction

"There are more things in heaven and Earth, Horatio, than are dreamt of in your philosophy.'

Hamlet—William Shakespeare

After a quarter of a century in the healing arts I am certain that the more I learn, the less I know and the more there is to be learned. Why do some people survive and others with the same disease perish? Why do some people succumb and others do not when an epidemic rages? Why do some people triumph in adversity and others cave in? Why do some people thrive on stress and others crumble under the weight? Why are some people strong and others weak?

Apart from all considerations of infection, inheritance, disease, environment, strength, weakness, nutrition, wealth or poverty there is the over-riding factor of spirit.

The key to good medicine is the consideration of that holy trinity, Body, Mind and Spirit, the platform on which Complementary Theraphy stands so firmly. Any practitioner who denies the intervention of some higher being in his healing work is supremely vain or insensitive. Intuition is not taught in medical schools but is a vital component in the armoury of the true "healer", even if he is unwilling to acknowledge this divine gift.

Today, alternative medicine is big business, and accounts

for millions of consultations each year. With the growth come the growing pains. The unscrupulous waiting to exploit the unwary. The back room bone setter with fancy diplomas. The part time accupuncturist and faithless faith healer. The public must be aware of this mushrooming industry and the dangers it brings.

The miracle of this book is the Miracle of Faith. Reading it you cannot fail to believe and be moved by the stories it unfolds. As a healer I am mystified. As a Dutch Jew, humbled by the courage of Aunty Cor and Opa—some of my own relations were hidden by a Catholic family during the war—and as a human being I am uplifted by the spiritual light in this book.

Martin Luther King said:

"The ultimate measure of a man is not where he stands in moments of comfort and convenience, but where he stands at times of challenge and controversy."

I have known Jan de Vries as a colleague and friend for many years, and there can be no question as to where he stands. It is firmly on the side of Holistic Medicine. He is a true "healer". He has the faith to help his patients help themselves to better health through a true understanding of the intricate balance between Body, Mind and Spirit.

Michael Van Straten
Cheddington
Bedfordshire

1

Are There Miracles?

EVER SINCE I was a child I have been intrigued by the subject of miracles. I have often tried to define for myself what a miracle *is*, as well as trying to find a definition for the actual word "miracle". Various dictionaries give different explanations of the word and some of those which appeal to me are the following:

> an extraordinary event manifesting divine intervention in human affairs;
>
> an event or action that apparently contradicts known scientific laws;
>
> a selection of the following: a marvellous, or extraordinary, or incredible, or supernatural, or unbelievable, or wonderful event.

My mother tongue, which is Dutch, again displays a diversity of meaning for the word "miracle". According to several dictionaries it can signify:

> an occurrence which is beyond human comprehension;
>
> an act of God which cannot be explained under the accepted rules and laws of nature;
>
> a divinely natural occurrence.

It seems that we have an enormously wide choice of words and phrases which are synonymous with the word "miracle". However, do miracles really exist and what *are* miracles? How many people have witnessed or experienced a miracle?

In order to find an answer to these questions I interviewed a large number of people, mainly my patients. I asked them if they had ever experienced or witnessed a miracle and unfortunately very few of them could give me either an affirmative or a satisfactory answer.

In my lifetime I have witnessed some miraculous events. Could any of these be classed as a miracle or might it be wiser to view these as events or occurrences for which no logical explanation exists?

When asking other people about miracles the answer I mostly received referred to the miracles which were performed in Biblical times, where the dead were brought back to life, those suffering from incurable diseases were cured, the blind were made to see and the deaf made to hear again. These were the miracles which Jesus Christ, the son of God, performed during His time on earth.

I was born and brought up in a strict Christian family and in my childhood I heard about these wonderful miracles. I often wondered why the dead could no longer be raised again as had happened in Biblical days. This question preyed on my mind a great deal. I was very young when my parents and I visited the home of an uncle who had died suddenly. The seeming finality of death began to bother me and rarely left my mind. My mother has since told me that at this time she was advised to take me away from the kindergarten I attended and have me enrolled in another school.

The educational system in the Netherlands differs quite considerably from that in the United Kingdom, in that public or private education is unusual. Primary as well as secondary education in the Netherlands is divided into state schools or what are called "Schools with the Bible". No religious instruction is given in state schools and the "School with the Bible" may belong to either a specific denomination or be classed merely as a Protestant or a Catholic school.

None of these schools would automatically fall into the fee-paying sector and parents are given a completely free choice. Even if the parents themselves are not religious, their children are still allowed to attend a "School with the Bible".

Because of the religious background of my family, I attended a kindergarten where Bible stories were part of the curriculum. Here it was noticed that the subject of death was becoming something of a phobia to me and my mother was advised to have me temporarily enrolled in a state school as the subject was just too emotive for my young and impressionable mind.

Thus I was moved to a state school. This did not stop me wondering, however, why no miracles took place like those we heard about when my mother read every morning from the Children's Bible.

I have no recollection of my problem at school, but what I can remember is the first instance when I thought a miracle had been performed. Although I considered it a miracle, it also frightened me badly at the time.

One of my young friends at primary school was allowed to invite a few lads to go for a day trip on his father's fishing boat and I was one of them. How it happened I cannot exactly remember, but one of the boys fell overboard. Eventually the crew was able to bring the boy back on board and we were badly shaken to see his lifeless body. We thought that our friend had drowned, but one of the fishermen told us that we had better pray very hard while they tried to revive the youngster by administering artificial respiration.

It was then that what I considered to be a miracle took place. We saw life returning to this boy and we all thanked God indeed for saving our friend. I remember how much of an impression this made on me and how I decided to keep my eyes open for other miracles, which of course did not happen.

I do believe, however, that God performed a miracle on the night when I was woken by unusual knocking sounds on my bedroom wall. As there were no neighbouring rooms, I could find no reason for these sounds, yet the knocking continued. Whatever was the cause, I still don't know, but it shocked me into the realisation that I was alone, which resulted in fear. I did not know what to do as the knocking persisted and I was too afraid to leave the room in the middle of the night.

I then remembered what my parents had taught me and I prayed to God to have this frightful sound stopped. While I prayed, the knocking kept on and became alternately louder and softer. There was an unnatural feeling in the room which I find very difficult to describe. Then suddenly I remembered, from the prayers which my mother had taught, the words: "I am always with you". All at once I felt as if God had spoken these words to me aloud there and then and I was comforted. The knocking eventually ceased. Since then, during some of the more difficult times of my life I have remembered and received solace from these words: "I am always with you".

I have had my share of difficult times and I sometimes think back to that fearful night in my childhood days. I then made a promise to God that I would honour him. Sadly I know I have not always kept that promise. I nevertheless know that God has always been with me and during any unusual event in my life, when I did not see a way out, or a solution myself, I have felt God's guidance.

I recall also the gradual process of my discovery of nature and how I considered that to be a miracle. I admired the wonders of nature—the flowers and plants, the animals and insects and all that nature offers. I slowly came to realise the force of nature in which we recognise the miracle of God's creation.

Another vivid memory I have is of going out to play with some friends. It was during the Second World War and as always we were very hungry. The harsh winter of 1944/5 is always referred to by the Dutch as the "hunger winter" and no mention of any year is necessary to indicate which period one is referring to. Without any real hope of finding anything, my friends and I looked around for something to eat, which had more or less become second nature.

Suddenly we spotted a German car. Nobody seemed to be about and as I was the smallest of our group I was chosen to investigate. What I found in that car was beyond belief: food, chocolate, sweets—to us it was like a miracle, this sheer abundance of food. I started throwing some of it out of the car, when suddenly one of the boys shouted that the British planes were coming over. Immediately all hell broke loose. We ran for our lives and jumped into a ditch to hide between the shrubs. There we kept our heads down and hoped that after finding that treasure trove, we would get the opportunity of taking advantage of it.

Thank goodness we had stuffed our pockets full before we made a dash for the ditch, because the car was hit and went up in flames. At least we had managed to salvage something. Was the timing of this air-raid pure coincidence? A few minutes sooner and we would have been killed, and some minutes later we would not have been aware of how near we had come to losing our lives!

On another occasion I also remember shouting at some German soldiers and pestering them. We were only young and if we had been alone we would not have dared, but each other's company gave us an inflated feeling of bravery. One of the soldiers turned and pointed his gun at us. We knew that life was of little value in those days and we had played foolishly with this precious gift. At that moment we realised only God could save us. He would either make the soldier shrug his shoulders and regard us as some foolish youngsters, or harden the soldier's mind to eliminate this disturbance. Anyhow, the soldier's attitude changed.

All these events together, some of more significance than others, made a lasting impression on me when I was young. I learned that we are protected by a Higher Power and that God is always with us. Often, though, when I realised how many civilians lost their lives, I asked myself the question: "Why them and not me?"

At this time, my mother was helping out with the nursing of the wounded in the danger zone around the Arnhem area.

Due to circumstances at home, she took me with her. Most people had been evacuated and we were aware of how precarious the situation was for civilians and prayed that God would protect us. He did!

With this childhood background my age group grew up quickly and learned faster about the realities of life than if it had been peacetime. I learned about life and death at an early age and events took place during my teenage years which made me look for the cause and effect of what happens in the world.

I discovered that we possess an immense power within ourselves to overcome problems. I learned that people, by prayer and faith, can overcome problems and illnesses and I also found that God supplies us with extraordinary mental and physical strength and power in times of need. This is apparent in the fact that when we suffer extreme pain, our body will release hormones which act as a natural morphine to relieve us.

I started looking for different types of miracle, or rather I started to look for miracles in different circumstances. Where before I had always considered the Biblical miracles as an example, I realised, that if we are prepared to see it that way, miracles or extraordinary events happen if only in the timing of everyday routine. Events take place which are inexplicable and afterwards they are often referred to as "fate".

During the days when I was working at Biohorma—a subsidiary of the Vogel laboratories in the Netherlands—I had to travel by train to The Hague once a week. It was a slightly complicated journey as there was no direct connection and I had to change trains along the way.

One morning my first train arrived slightly ahead of schedule, which enabled me to catch an earlier connection to my destination. I had to sprint, but it was worthwhile as I arrived at the Biohorma offices in The Hague well ahead of my usual time.

These few minutes at the change-over saved me quite a bit of time. However, it most likely also saved my life. About an hour after my arrival in The Hague the telephone rang and Mr Bolle, the present Director of Biohorma, anxiously asked our assistant to tell him quickly if I had arrived.

From him we learned that the train in which I would have been travelling under normal circumstances had been involved in a very serious rail accident. Indeed, this is considered to be one of the worst ever accidents in the history of the Dutch railways. More phone calls followed, as both my wife and my mother knew that I normally would have caught that train. I could only thank God from the bottom of my heart that I was still alive. I asked myself if this was a miracle, or was it merely the case that circumstances had been in my favour.

In the Bible we read in the book of Ecclesiastes (9: 11-12):

> In this world fast runners do not always win the race. The brave do not always win the battle. Wise men do not always earn a living. Intelligent men do not always get rich. Capable men do not always rise to high positions. Time and unforeseen occurrences befall them all. You never know when your time is coming. Like birds suddenly caught in a trap, like fish caught in a net, we are trapped at some evil moment when we least expect it.

In the case of some persons in early Biblical history the general pattern of their birth and life was prophesied, although many incidents in their lives seemed due to time and unforeseen or unforeseeable circumstances. Nevertheless, experiences like my speedy train journey—and its fortunate consequences—are the result of unusual situations and we can only be grateful for such benefits.

It is interesting to see that while many of the miracles recorded in the Old Testament of the Bible, like that of the Israelites crossing the Red Sea, could possibly be explained by some natural phenomenon, the miracles which were performed in the New Testament are beyond explanation. An example of this is the miraculous awakening of Lazarus from the dead (John 11: 39). Even so, attempts are often made to explain it by the possibility that Lazarus could have been in a coma. However, if we actually read the account in the Bible we find that it tells us of "the smell of death".

Dealing with so many patients, I often hear such statements as: "It was like a miracle" or "you have performed a miracle". I can honestly say that in the majority of cases the explanation is simply a matter of cause and effect.

Physically, mentally and spiritually we see a world before us which awaits exploration by our thoughts and action. Our actions may be influenced by our thoughts and our minds. Cause and effect is truly the law of the universe because God's power is seen in heaven and earth in its entirety. If we recognise Him as our Creator, we will find that His laws can can be expressed in many ways.

At school we learned that for every action there is an equal and opposite reaction. Due to the activity of our mind and our thoughts, ideas come to life. With the reality of everyday life, we also learn to accept the universal laws of cause and effect.

God has created us so that we are free in our thoughts and in our choices, making us capable of doing things in life which are most important to us. Let us therefore be a credit to Him and follow the laws of nature, which are the laws of God.

Because we are all imperfect, we all have some health problems. This may be due to adverse reactions to our thoughts and deeds. However, if we decide to live according to the laws of nature, this negative reaction could be transformed and would have a positive effect on our well-being.

Nature is such a tremendous form of energy. It brings God's laws into operation and covers so many different aspects. By obeying His laws our lives may serve as a credit to our Creator.

Activity and energy is often on our minds and we tend to act according to our convictions. If we think positively, we may *expect* to find a positive answer or resolution, while to others the eventual outcome may be viewed as a miracle.

Is it not a miracle when we see how from small and seemingly insignificant seeds, large and strong trees grow? Therefore the seeds of energy, which God has given us by His creative power, can be used to help others.

Negative thinking will get us nowhere. It will be the cause of failure and of many unhappy moments in our lives. The minute we replace a negative thought with a positive thought, we experience as it were, a small miracle. Life creates wonderful chances and opportunities in which to show the miracle of God's nature. This spirit I have seen especially strong in those people we might refer to as "uncivilised". They seem to be more capable of living in peace and harmony with nature.

Impossibilities will become possible if we have an enthusiastic and positive mind. It is often said that we live in difficult times, yet this could be the most marvellous time to prove ourselves and the principles in which we believe, and to develop a positive attitude to all problems.

God has given us three sources of energy, i.e. food, water and air. It is our duty to keep these sources free from contamination and as natural as possible, and doing so will consequently influence our energy outflow.

I once attended a course in a specific branch of natural medicine as part of a group of twelve. I was puzzled when, towards the end of the course, two of us were singled out by the professor who had been in charge of this course. He asked us if we had noticed that we had achieved better successes in treating our patients than the other students, and wondered if we knew why this should be the case. As we had no idea why this should be so, he told us that a positive attitude seemed to emanate from us to the good of the patient. Somehow or another we managed to conduct this feeling to our patients, who seemed to react positively to it and for that reason benefited.

This positive energy is a gift of God, which has enabled me to help thousands of people. This, coupled with the love and interest I have for helping people, has been the reason why I have been able to perform what some people have called miracles, but what I attribute to the law of cause and effect.

We are aware that we cannot cure. God cures and we can only try to heal by pointing out possibilities and encouraging people to help themselves, using this immense power and life force within ourselves, which is beyond human explanation.

It is a field which is so wide, that it can only be discovered if we take time to think about it and to use it unselfishly.

Are there miracles or is there any explanation for miracles? Looking at the various definitions for the word "miracle", which I have listed at the beginning of this chapter, we have each to find the answer for ourselves.

I have heard many stories which have inspired me to search for a definition myself. In the next chapter I would like to relate a story, one of many stories about the way God showed his extraordinary powers during the war. It gives us an insight into what may be expected if a positive mind goes into action. When everything in life seems lost, it is astonishing to see how, by unforeseen action, God will undertake and perform what might conceivably be regarded as a miracle.

On 16 August 1942 in the *Observer*, W. J. Brown wrote in the column "Sayings of the Week": "We have not yet lost this war, but we are overdrawn on the bank of miracles."

2

The Hidden Village—a Miracle?

IN JUNE 1971 a reporter from one of the local papers wrote in his column "Going places—Meeting people" that he was looking forward to meeting an elderly Dutch widow who was due to arrive in Troon shortly. He was interested to hear more of her remarkable story about a secret village she had helped to run in the Netherlands during the Second World War, where refugees from the German regime were hidden.

The lady in question was Mrs Christina Bakker, one of the leaders of this secret village, established in the woods outside Nunspeet, a small community about one hour's drive from Amsterdam.

Mrs Bakker, generally known in the Resistance movement as Aunty Cor, was badly in need of rest and this was the reason why we had brought her over to our residential clinic in Troon, Scotland. She was feeling very low when I had last seen her in the Netherlands, so I told her that a few months with us in Scotland would do her the world of good. We were very fond of Aunty Cor and knew of the torture she had been put through when the Germans killed her husband only just before the end of the war.

She had never fully regained her health, which had

suffered badly when she heard that her husband had been killed, and she found it difficult to talk about the exceptional work she and her husband had undertaken in the secret village.

Events had taken place there which defy sensible explanation, for significant, extraordinary powers had shown themselves to be at work. It would, therefore, be worthwhile spending a section of this book on one of the many stories which happened during the Second World War in my motherland, the Netherlands.

About six miles outside the little town of Nunspeet in the middle of the Netherlands, there is a forest. The Soerelse Bossen is not an exceptionally large forest, nor a particularly well known one, yet it holds a special place in the hearts of hundreds of people.

In the middle of this forest stands a boulder; again, just an ordinary looking boulder. Ordinary that is, until you see the plaque which has been attached to it. The boulder is in fact a monument to the courage and the fortitude of the Dutch people of that area, who, during the Second World War, hid many Jews, resistance fighters and allied airmen from the might of Nazi Germany.

Despite a very real risk of discovery, which would have automatically resulted in execution, the townspeople of Nunspeet built a secret village in the middle of the pine forest and there they hid as many fugitives from the Nazi regime as they could.

The story of how this hidden village was conceived, organised and eventually discovered, is human and touching. At times it is either tragic or comical, but throughout it is completely true and that is what makes it worth telling. The village was built on love, unity and trust, even though at that time the world was on fire. Hundreds of people from different walks of life and backgrounds were joined together by a single bond—hatred of a common enemy and fear of discovery.

The fact that so many people could be hidden for almost

three years in the middle of an occupied country is a *miracle*. But probably the most miraculous and heartening aspect of the whole incident is that although most of the 800 inhabitants of Nunspeet knew about the secret village in the woods, not one of them betrayed its existence.

A great example for the world of today. No word of political disputes, no religious problems. In one spirit and without fear they worked against the enemy, towards the victory which they knew would come. Is this perhaps a clue to one of the reasons why our generation is disillusioned? Have we not yet learned how to live in peace and to look at some of the miraculous events which take place in everyday life, despite two world wars?

On Monday, 4 May 1970, it was my privilege to be present when the monument was unveiled in the Soerelse Bossen. The unveiling ceremony was a simple one and the monument itself was no more than a boulder bearing a small plaque. Yet that simple monument marks the spot where one of the most incredible and intriguing dramas of World War II was acted out. So many Dutch patriots, Jews, British and American airmen, even Russian prisoners of war were hidden there in underground huts. Some remained hidden there for years, despite all-out efforts by the German Wehrmacht to find them. Others stayed there for shorter periods on their way to other safe places or back across the water.

The guest of honour at the unveiling ceremony was the small, frail-looking Aunty Cor, together with another guest—a robust elderly gentleman called Leen, who viewed the ceremony from a wheelchair. Not only had Aunty Cor herself played a leading role in the founding and running of this hidden village, but her husband, Opa Bakker, had been the inspiration and main driving force behind it.

When the unveiling ceremony was over and the crowd began to disperse, Aunty Cor went over to her husband's grave. Earlier, she had placed a wreath there, but now as she stood alone, looking down at the flowers and the headstone, her eyes misted over and her mind slipped back through the years to those dark days of 1940-45.

She recollected how, on a cold winter's night in 1941, the two of them had been sitting at a roaring log-fire in their cottage and she had asked her husband if he would like some coffee. He had nodded and stared into the fire. He seemed preoccupied and she had known instantly that something was not right.

Slowly he responded to her questions of what was wrong and he told her that he had been talking to some friends down at the market place, from whom he had heard about some of the terrible things which were happening. He had been told how the Germans were treating the Jewish people, herding them together and transporting them in cattle trains to Poland where a horrible death awaited them. He felt compelled to ease their frightful predicament.

What could they do? If they were found assisting Jews, they would both immediately be shot. Nevertheless, Opa Bakker maintained that it was their duty to help and fight the Germans.

The conversation petered out there, but a short while later Opa caught the train to Amsterdam where he contacted some friends whom he knew had joined the Resistance movement. He was determined to do what he considered his duty and save as many Jews from certain death at the hands of the Nazis and it was arranged that his Resistance friends would meet him soon near Nunspeet.

What part should Opa play? How should he go about contacting Jews who needed to go underground? He could not very well advertise his willingness and services; and where would he find safe hiding places?

So many questions and problems arose and he felt a novice, slowly having to feel his way, picking people's brains and asking for advice. At times it seemed a virtual impossibility to know who to include in his plans. Everything had to be done in utter secrecy.

Opa met again with his friends from the Resistance just outside Nunspeet and they started to make concrete plans.

How careful they had to be, because German spies or Nazi sympathisers might be encountered everywhere and one was bound to be caught if every possible care was not taken. Even then the dangers were real enough.

One evening, Opa was secretly approached by a contact and asked to hide two Jews, as their situation had become precarious. The fugitives arrived shortly after midnight and, as they had not eaten for several days, they considered the food prepared by Aunty Cor a godsend. After they had eaten, Opa quietly hid the two Jews in a chicken coop in the backyard, which had been especially prepared as a hide-out.

It was only a matter of time before more people who had been forced to go underground found their way to them. They would have liked to share their house with the fugitives, but they knew the danger of prying eyes and realised that some people would have no qualms in reporting them to the authorities.

And sure enough, when Opa was down at the market one day, he heard the whispered warning: "The Germans are on to you. Be careful!" Feeling utterly confused because he could not work out who had warned him, he returned home and told Aunty Cor what had happened and that they had better be extra careful.

It was then that Aunty Cor and Opa Bakker, as they were referred to by most people in those days, experienced the first miracle. Not long after Opa's warning, in the middle of the night, they heard a car stop outside the house. Aunty Cor awoke instantly. She asked softly if Opa had heard the car as well. He shushed her and told her to keep quiet. Opa was frightened, but realised that the worst thing they could do was to panic. For months he had dreaded this moment, often wondering how he would react when it finally came to the crunch.

His wife could sense his fear and she placed a reassuring hand on his shoulder. "Put your trust in God," she said, "and everything will work out all right."

Suddenly there was a hard knock on the door and Aunty Cor told her husband to go and answer it. If the Germans were there to arrest them, at least they would go together, because she would never leave him. The hammering on the door became more impatient. Opa threw an old coat over his shoulders and went down quickly to open the door.

When he pushed back the iron bolts and swung the wooden door open, he found himself staring straight down the barrel of a Luger automatic.

As a soldier in the First World War Opa had seen guns before and they held no special fear for him, but the ice-cold eyes of the blond Aryan officer holding the pistol and the "SS" patches on the lapels of his uniform were, to the Dutchman, like a bucket of freezing water thrown over a drunken man.

If Opa had ever had any ideas about reckless courage when in the grip of danger, they vanished in a flash. There was no mercy whatsoever in the face of the Nazi before him. Opa would have to play things carefully, very carefully indeed. The German officer in charge pushed him into the house and demanded to know why he had taken so long to answer their summons.

Opa stammered that he had been asleep, to which the German sneered: "That is what is wrong with you pigs. You are always asleep. You were asleep when we conquered you and you sleep while we rule you."

Opa was infuriated, but he kept his mouth shut. Maybe it was better if the Germans thought that the Dutch people had accepted their defeat. Silently though, he thought to himself how glad he was that he and others had realised some possibilities of fighting back. Their country might be overrun, but the Dutch people were not defeated.

He asked the German what he wanted and was totally ignored by the officer, who ordered his men to search the house. They turned the place upside down.

The SS officer grabbed Opa and shoved him into the backyard.

"Where are the Jews?" he demanded, a fanatical gleam in his eye.

"What are you talking about?" asked Opa. He was frightened but, paradoxically, he drew strength from the fact that he was aware of his fear.

The SS officer slapped Opa hard across the mouth and screamed: "Swine! There are Jews here, I know it. I will find them and then I will shoot you. Your wife may take a little longer to die!"

Then his face lit up when he saw the chicken coops. He swaggered across and, with a sly glint in his eyes, he asked Opa what was in them.

"Chickens and hens," replied the old Dutchman.

The German ordered his men to search the coops, but they found nothing. He was beginning to get frustrated, as he had already searched several houses that week and had come away empty-handed every time. He began to pace up and down, flashing his torch at the hedge behind the chicken coops.

Opa's breath stopped. The summer house behind the hedge was concealing fourteen Jews. If the Germans decided to search it, all would be lost. Just as the German officer seemed to notice the summer house, however, there came from a distance the noise of many aircraft flying in formation. The drone gradually grew louder and the Germans looked up. The aircraft were Royal Air Force bombers on their way to devastate the Ruhr area, the heart of industrial Germany.

Quickly the officer ordered his men to put out their lights. He was disgusted with yet another failure but thought that he had better get his men back to barracks, in case they were needed if a British bomber were shot down in the area. So, only stopping to curse Opa and the whole Dutch nation, he regrouped his men, marched them back to their truck and drove off.

Opa could not believe his luck and he rushed back to his wife to tell her what had happened. Aunty Cor, when she saw her husband, began to cry, purely from relief. Rushing over to Opa, she threw her arms around him and thanked

God for performing a miracle, for seeing them through the danger.

This incident involving the chicken coop underlined the necessity of finding safe hiding-places for the fugitives. Opa knew that he could not go on indefinitely, shifting the 14 Jews from the chicken coops to the summer house and back again. He had fooled the Germans once, but knew they were not stupid and would be back. Opa realised that he might not be so lucky the next time.

He began to think seriously about arranging a more secure hideout. The more he thought about it, the more he became convinced that the nearby forest would be an ideal location.

He thought of the caravan which was hidden in the forest by some of the Resistance men. There a whole Jewish family had found refuge. He had actually visited them on a number of occasions, taking food, information and the odd newspaper along with him.

The caravan had been in the forest for quite a while now and the six Jews were still living a comparatively safe existence in their "underground" home. Granted, they could think of more comfortable conditions, but this was a small price to pay for their lives.

How the caravan had come to be established in the woods was an exceptional story and Opa knew all the facts, although he had not actually been involved himself.

One of the villagers had known of the large ancient caravan which had stood virtually unused in someone's yard for many years. He and some others intended to buy this caravan and tow it to a glen in the forest about six miles out of town. There they hoped to use the caravan to hide a Jewish family from the Germans.

The owner of the caravan was approached with a view to buying the vehicle. The Resistance man explained that he was selling his house and needed the caravan to transport his belongings. The caravan owner, however, informed him that the caravan was not for sale. The prospective buyer appealed to him that it was needed desperately and that the owner never used it anyway.

"No, I have told you, it is not for sale. Now get off my land," was the final answer.

The Resistance man, incensed by the offhand rejection of his request, angrily shouted that unless the man sold him the caravan he would be responsible for the deaths of six people. The owner was visibly taken aback by this accusation and he asked what it was supposed to mean. The Resistance man decided on impulse that the caravan owner could be trusted.

"I will tell you the truth, why I really need the caravan, and then I will ask you again to sell it."

He then related the story of how his group were trying to save the lives of a family of Dutch Jews, who had been forced to disappear from sight. The man immediately agreed to give his caravan to the Resistance and apologised for not doing so in the first place.

The troubles really started, however, when they tried to move the caravan on to the main road. The men had brought two horses with them to tow the caravan, but had badly underestimated the weight of the old, solid iron vehicle. The horses strained and the men pushed, but the caravan would not move an inch. Their carefully worked out plan seemed to have been scuppered by a foolish oversight.

Then they thought of using the tractor and at last the horses, together with the tractor, managed to pull the old caravan out on to the road and they made their way to where the refugees were waiting.

All six members of the Jewish family were hidden in the caravan and set off for the forest. Everything seemed to be going well when, only a mile away from the safety of the woods, they were stopped by a German patrol.

If the Germans decided to search the caravan all would be lost and the men, although trying hard to look as normal and unconcerned as possible, were sick with fear. The officer in charge of the patrol strutted towards them and demanded to know what was in the caravan. Only quick thinking saved them.

"There is nothing in the caravan but our personal effects. Our house is now serving as a billet for German officers. We have been thrown out and have decided to move to another district." The German soldiers laughed, but they seemed to be satisfied with the reply. Anyway, the officer in charge decided not to search the caravan and, appearing to be in a hurry, marched his men away, muttering curses under his breath to them in particular and to the Dutch people in general.

At this, the blood of the Resistance men boiled and only a restraining hand and a sense of self-preservation stopped them from chasing after the Germans. It would not only be their own lives which would be forfeited, but the lives of the six Jews as well. As they watched the German soldiers retreating down the road, they breathed a sigh of relief and once again the strange procession started on its way towards the forest.

Just as they turned off the main road on to the track which led directly into the forest, the caravan slewed sideways and slithered into the ditch. The Jews inside the caravan were startled by the jolt and the head of the family, a white-haired old man in his late sixties, came out to see what was happening.

The Resistance men were terrified that the German patrol might come back along the road and immediately sent the old man back into the caravan.

"For God's sake, stay out of sight until we get this thing back on the road and into the woods," he was told. But that was easier said than done.

For almost an hour they struggled to try and get the heavy caravan out of the ditch, but despite the combined efforts of the three men, two horses and the tractor; it remained stuck. The men were shattered. All their planning, precautions and courage had been wasted by a careless accident! They sat down and tried to think out their next move.

One thing was certain: they could not just walk away and leave the Jews to their fate. Nor could they spend much more time trying to get the caravan out of the ditch, as the German patrol was very likely to come back along that road. On the other hand, they could hardly leave the caravan where it was in case the authorities started asking awkward questions. The situation certainly seemed hopeless.

At that moment the old Jew came out of the caravan again and walked up to the men. He was looking desperately worried: "Please can I do anything to help? If the Germans find us here, we will all be lost. They will kill me and my family and you as well, thanks to your kindness to us."

As the men were now growing impatient with fear and worry, he was asked in a rather derisive manner whatever he thought *he* could do to solve their predicament. "We have tried to put the caravan back on to the road and we cannot. Even the horses and the tractor cannot get it out of that ditch."

The old man looked steadily at his helpers. "Please," he whispered, "please, we have come this far and we cannot fail now. Not when safety is almost in our grasp. We must get that caravan out of the ditch."

They had abstractly noticed that the old man's voice had increased in pitch towards the end of his short speech. They looked inquisitively at the small, frail Jew and for the first time saw the grim determination burning behind the sorrow in his tired old eyes.

But even then, they were still astounded when the old man slowly took off his jacket and, without saying a word, turned towards the caravan. They all watched the Jew with a mixture of humour, amazement and fear—the latter because at any moment a German soldier or a Dutch collaborator might pass by.

The old man stopped at the side of the caravan and stared at it. To the onlookers it seemed as if he was looking at the caravan without actually seeing it. There was a far-away expression on his face. The Jew then looked up at the sky, muttered something, bent down and took hold of the bottom of the caravan.

"He is going to lift it out himself," the men whispered to each other . . . and the smile died on their lips as the old Jew did exactly that. He succeeded, where the combined efforts of three men, two horses and a tractor had failed. The small, frail Jew had lifted the caravan out of the ditch and placed it firmly back on the road.

After completing this superhuman act the old man sank to his knees and prayed. The Resistance men were literally struck dumb. They could not believe what they had just witnessed, yet there was the proof in front of them—the caravan was back on the road.

"A miracle!" they whispered. "We have just witnessed a miracle." The men knelt on the ground and thanked God for His help in this hour of need. "Come on, grab the old man and let us get out of here," they shouted. And although they had been able to do little more than stand staring in amazement at the old man, they got themselves into action. They helped the Jew back into the caravan and set off into the woods.

To this day, the men involved are still awed by this particular incident and continue to refer to it as a miracle.

Not long after entering the comparative safety of the woods, the procession reached the specially chosen place, a hollow which had been deepened and prepared in advance, where the caravan was to be hidden. The spot was ideal, well away from the main paths and tracks, not easily accessible and near to a freshwater stream. Once the caravan was in the hollow, its roof was just about level with the ground. The men quickly covered the whole vehicle with pine cones and needles until it was completely camouflaged.

In fact, the caravan was hidden so well that, unless one knew where to look, it was almost entirely invisible from the ground as well as from the air. This was soon put to the test when, a few days later, a British fighter plane was shot down over Nunspeet and wreckage was scattered all over the forest.

Almost immediately the woods were swarming with Germans who were thoroughly searching the whole area for vital components or for information which they thought the aircraft might have been carrying. But despite their painstaking search they did not find the caravan nor its Jewish occupants. One German patrol even walked right alongside it without noticing. Even though the Resistance men did not know it at the time, this was the beginning of an underground community where so many people would remain hidden from the Germans.

While the story about this caravan kept turning around in Opa's mind, he gradually reached a decision. It was slow in coming, for the old Dutchman liked to examine an idea from every angle. In his mind he debated the plan, working out its chances of success and failure. He sought every possible flaw in it and devised solutions to overcome them. Eventually he came up with what he believed was a foolproof plan—or at least as nearly foolproof as any plan could be.

If one caravan could remain hidden in the woods for so long, so could other caravans or huts, if they were concealed in the same way. Opa's scheme was to dig holes, deep in the soft ground near the centre of the forest, shore up the sides with timber and lay thick planks across the top. Turf, pine-needles and logs could be laid over these planks so that the huts would be concealed from even the most determined searchers. It would have to be so well concealed that people walking or standing on top of the underground huts would never guess that they existed. The camouflage would have to be perfect—anything less would spell disaster.

Opa carefully worked out his next moves. First on his list of priorities was to find a suitable location for the huts, and to do this he had to get into the forest without arousing suspicion. Normally when he visited the Jewish family in the caravan he travelled at night, taking care that no one followed him into the woods or spied on him on the way. However, if he was to obtain a clear picture of the forest and find the best possible hiding place, he would have to go in daylight. This would be more difficult.

It was Aunty Cor who eventually, more by accident than

design, came up with a solution. One night after supper, Opa was sitting at the fireside, pondering over his plans to build the underground huts, when Aunty Cor—who had been busy clearing away the dishes in the kitchen—asked him if he would like to go into the country somewhere for a picnic in the near future.

He replied absent-mindedly, not really hearing her, that he thought that was not a bad idea. Then he slowly began to realise just what his wife had said and it dawned on him how good an idea it really was. He ran over to his wife, swept her into his arms and showered her with kisses. He shouted: "Cor, you are really marvellous!"

"But I only suggested going for a picnic!" she laughed. "I dread to think what you would have done if I had suggested a six-course banquet."

"No, you don't understand. We can go to the forest for a picnic and at the same time I can look for a site where I can build a hiding place for the Jews. It is spring and it is not unusual to go out for a picnic at this time of year. If the Germans see us they will probably think we are no more than two old fools trying to recapture the joys of youth," enthused Opa.

The Soerelse Bossen is a fairly large forest and Opa knew that they would not have time to inspect it as thoroughly as he would have wished. Nevertheless, in the short time available, he was determined to find a spot where his plan could become reality.

As it turned out on the day, it was very much easier than he had dared to hope. He had noticed a rabbit scampering through a thick clump of bushes and on impulse he decided to follow it. He crawled through a small gap in the bushes, cursing as thorns scratched his face and tore at his clothes. But he forgot all this discomfort when he saw the hollow clearing, which hitherto had been hidden by the bushes. It was ideal—large enough to accommodate a fair number of underground huts and yet small enough to be hidden without too much difficulty.

The clearing was not easily accessible—as Opa could readily testify—therefore picnickers and passers-by would be unlikely to use it. Even the majority of Nazi patrols would probably give it no more than a perfunctory glance through the bushes and, on seeing nothing out of order, forget about it. Other patrols would possibly send a man into the clearing to inspect it, but he would most likely be a raw recruit, and that recruit, after hearing his mates laugh as he squirmed through the narrow gap in the bushes, would be too embarrassed and angry to inspect the clearing properly.

Opa smiled as he surveyed the clearing with his practised engineer's eye. There was only one flaw . . . he had found the clearing too easily. At that moment he became aware that someone was standing behind him. He whirled round and was surprised to see his wife just a few yards away. She must have come in through the same gap as Opa, but seemed unmarked by the thorns.

To his enquiries as to how she got in, she replied: "Same way as you, but remember I am smaller than you and it was easier for me."

Opa smiled and took his wife's hand. "Look at this clearing," he said softly. "It is ideal for the purpose, yet finding it was almost too easy."

"If it was easy, then it was because God helped you to find it," Aunty Cor replied. "This clearing is the right place for the huts. I know it. I can feel it in my bones that this is the right place for your secret village."

Opa thought aloud: "Secret village or hidden village. I have never considered it as such. Yet, I suppose that is what it will be. A village hidden in the woods, where hunted people from all over the country can come and hide from the Nazis. A place where they can at least have company, shelter, a measure of freedom and as much security as we can give them. Yes, a secret village . . . that is how we will hit back at the Germans. We will help to save as many lives as possible of our countrymen and allies alike."

He kissed his wife and then they left to return home. Now

the time had come to study the aetails of the plans Opa had worked out in his mind.

Gradually, forest workers and farmers—men who could be trusted—were recruited to boost the workforce. It was a critical period, but the plan for the hidden village met with such wholehearted approval that everyone involved got caught up in their enthusiasm and forgot all their doubts. Between them they had no trouble in recruiting trustworthy men.

Lack of money was another problem to be faced. None of them was rich, but fate played a hand. Mr Boem, a kind gentleman who felt sympathetic towards the plight of the Jews and who was actually hiding some Jews himself in his large house on the outskirts of the town, answered their prayers. He helped wherever he could.

Slowly the village began to grow. More pits were dug, 12-feet deep, 12-feet wide and 12-feet long. The work was hard and backbreaking and would have been difficult enough under normal circumstances. Considering the complications arising out of the need for secrecy, the task was almost impossible. The spades and pickaxes needed for the job had all to be smuggled into the forest on a handcart and had been concealed there.

The workers built wooden bunks into the walls of the four huts and these huts were becoming quite nice and cosy. The next stage of the operation was by far the most difficult and dangerous one. They had to move forty-eight Jewish men and women out of their hiding places in the village and take them to the forest six miles away. This had to be done in total secrecy.

Aunty Cor will never forget one particular old Jewish gentleman who, before the war, had been a respected doctor in Amsterdam. He took her hands and with tears in his eyes he whispered his gratitude. "Thank you, thank you," he said, choking with emotion. "You have given us hope and you have given us life. Here we may yet escape the clutches of those Nazi madmen who seem so bent on destroying our race."

Another of the fugitives, a young man, even managed to raise a feeble joke about the situation—despite the desperate plight he and his companions were in. "It is certainly not the best establishment I have stayed in," he quipped. But he forestalled any laughter by adding more seriously, "though I suppose it will be more comfortable than a cattle truck to a Polish or German concentration camp."

Looking after the health of the people of the secret village was also a great responsibility, but nature was a wonderful help and they used as many natural remedies as possible. That, coupled with the selflessness, courage and co-operation of a village doctor and dentist, ensured that all the fugitives were well cared for. Those reliable people had readily agreed to give their services when they had been approached and they frequently visited the village to give treatment to those who needed it.

Food for the inhabitants was another major problem. Food was fast becoming a luxury and many people went hungry despite the fact that they had ration-books and food coupons, because these only covered the bare minimum. Although many people helped and food was frequently smuggled into the village, things became more and more difficult as the population increased, at times reaching almost one hundred.

In 1944 the Germans became more desperate. On one occasion when Aunty Cor had returned home from trying to obtain counterfeit food coupons and ration books, she was very depressed. She had been to visit my birthplace, Kampen, and there she heard that one of the greatest Resistance members had been shot while trying to escape by way of the river.

Although I myself was still very young, I do remember how people went around the town, crying in public. This great man, who had symbolised freedom to so many people, was shot in cold blood by the Nazis, along with so many others.

Not long afterwards, the "Massacre of Putten" took place when the whole male population of that town were either executed or transported to German camps. Putten was a nearby village and actually not far from the secret hiding place in the forest. Yet again, in among all that misery in the village of Putten, one occasion stood out which can only be considered a miracle, as many lives were saved after all.

Towards the end of the war the Germans by no means softened their attitude. Their reprisals against the actions of partisans or the underground movement were terrible and ensured that people would not lose sight of the harsh reality.

Four high-ranking German officers had been travelling by car from Apeldoorn to Putten when, as they rounded a bend on the outskirts of Putten, they struck a land mine which had been planted there by Dutch partisans. Two of the officers were killed instantly and the other two were shot as they tried to scramble clear of the wreckage.

The Nazi revenge was swift and terrible. Within hours of the incident an SS unit isolated Putten and the inhabitants were warned that all 8,000 of them would be put to death if those responsible for killing the officers did not give themselves up or were handed over. The Dutch townspeople knew only too well the atrocities of which the SS were capable and that the Nazis were not bluffing. Yet they refused to give any relevant information.

Incensed by the lack of co-operation, the German commanding officer ordered that some of the town's leading citizens be hanged in the market square. The executions were carried out thirty-six hours after the German staff car was blown up. Every man, woman and child in Putten was ordered to witness this reprisal action. This atrocity still did not break the spirit of the villagers and they resolutely maintained their silence.

The SS commander, a vicious, ruthless man even by Nazi standards, was determined to get the information he required. He had all the men in the town arrested and when he realised that no one was going to betray the local Resistance groups, he had them all transported to death camps or labour camps in Germany. His anger was still not spent.

The SS commander was intent on making an example of the village of Putten. By exacting a terrible revenge he hoped to show the rest of the country the futility of such obstinacy. He ordered his men to round up the remainder of the population: the women and children were to be assembled in the local church. He then withdrew the major part of his unit from the town, leaving a small force behind with orders to burn down the church.

The Nazis piled petrol-soaked straw around the church and set it alight, but although the blaze blackened and scarred the stone walls, the church itself miraculously did not catch fire. Inside the church the women and children kept calm and prayed, while outside the Germans became more and more frustrated and frantic in their ineffective efforts to burn down the old building. Eventually the SS detachment gave up and, to save themselves further embarrassment, hastily left the town. Indeed, a miracle had taken place!

The inhumanity of the deed they had attempted to commit was of no consequence to the Nazis. Possibly their only regret was that they had no explosives with which they might have blown up the church. A conscience was something which SS men were not required to possess and they feared the disapproval of their superior officers more than they feared the wrath of God.

A few hours after the Germans had left Putten, a group of Resistance men arrived who freed the women and children from the church building.

It was a solemn procession which emerged from the church, after offering up a prayer of thanks to God for their salvation. They were too full of sorrow to celebrate their escape. They had watched their fathers, brothers, husbands and sons being marched away to their likely deaths in Germany and they had cradled their young innocent children in their arms as the Nazis tried to burn them alive. Emotionally they were drained, their minds void of all feeling. Soon the full horror of what had happened in Putten during those few fateful days would dawn on them and they would become angry, bitter and sad, but their spirit would remain undampened and their belief in final victory unchanged.

When the Dutch population heard of the tragedy which had taken place in Putten, they became very conscious that there was still a long, weary and bloody path ahead of them before peace and sanity returned to their country.

The inhabitants of the hidden village did not hear of the Massacre of Putten until after the Germans had left the stricken town. They were in the middle of a meeting at the hidden village, when a Resistance member arrived and tearfully told them what had happened.

Their first reactions were ones of despair and futility, but like those who themselves had survived the massacre, their grim determination to fight on increased and they were prepared wherever possible to double their efforts to struggle through to final victory and freedom.

Maintaining the safety of the village if something was to happen was a great worry. At one point when they were afraid that news about the village might have leaked out, the leaders had the whole village evacuated in no time at all. They tried to be prepared for anything unforeseen.

Numerous stories and anecdotes exist about this village and some of the happenings are frequently referred to as miracles by those who were involved. One of the most amazing facts, however, was that the feared Rauter, the same man who ordered the Massacre of Putten, looked for the village everywhere, but even with 500 German troops he was not able to find it. It had actually happened that Rauter himself walked right over the huts together with two Gestapo officers and they never knew.

When the end came, it was sudden and unnecessary.

Two of the younger boys who were hidden in the village had left to collect some firewood. Unfortunately they went slightly further out from their site than necessary and encountered two German soldiers who were just walking about. They were not looking for anything in particular and if the boys had not panicked, possibly nothing untoward would have happened. However, when the boys saw the Germans they screamed: "Germans, Germans!" and ran back to their hiding place. The soldiers only followed the lads far enough to see where they were heading for and then left for reinforcements.

Sunday, 29 October 1944, was the sad day on which the hidden village was discovered. Within the briefest span of time the whole village was emptied. When the Germans returned in strength, nearly everybody was out. Eight people in total lost their lives.

One family had returned to collect some of their treasured possessions, despite the fact that Aunty Cor had given everyone express instructions to leave any valuables in safe-keeping at the bank or with friends, and not to bring them into hiding with them. It was thought that everybody had obeyed these instructions and that they had taken the advice so as not to be encumbered by too many possessions. This family, however, had lacked faith and paid dearly for their mistrust. On their return to the village they walked straight into the arms of the Germans and were shot on the spot.

Some others were found in one of the houses where they had temporarily gone to ground, waiting for exigency plans to go into action and new hiding places to be found for them. A few others were unfortunately spotted on their way to a new "safe house".

Yet, of all those people who had been living in the underground village, only eight were caught by the Germans during the enforced rearrangements. Among the Resistance people the village was known by the apt name "Pas Op Kamp", which means the "Be Aware Camp".

An incredible piece of history came to an end when this wonderful work of unity and love was sadly discontinued. Yet, was it not a miracle that nearly everyone who lived in the village at that time was saved?

During the unveiling ceremony of the monument, I spoke with a young doctor who was present there and he told me that he had been one of the youngest inhabitants of the camp.

He related some of his memories and experiences which would be part of him for the rest of his life and how often he had heard the words: "The job must be done!"

He also remembered sleeping in a bottom bunk, the bunk above his being occupied by an elderly Jewish gentleman. Occasionally this gentleman seemed to suffer from lack of bladder control and the young doctor could remember being woken at odd times during the night due to slight mishaps above him!

The small monument, erected on the site of the secret village, will serve as a reminder that, due to a combination of hard physical work, faith and prayer, achievements were obtained there which had been undreamed of previously.

Because of the secret nature of the village, very few photographs are available. Those which are printed on the cover of this book, however, may give some indication of the conditions which prevailed. Also, seeing these photographs may stir the memories of a doctor who, according to the latest information, is at present working in Scotland as a surgeon. Those people in Nunspeet who were involved and are still alive have lost touch with him, but the sight of these photographs may remind that doctor of those years spent in the secrecy of an underground village.

3

Can Faith, Prayer or Meditation
Perform Miracles?

Faith

IN THE PREVIOUS chapter we have read how much may be achieved by positive faith, creating the impression that through true faith and prayer seemingly impossible goals were achieved.

Depending on which dictionary we use to look up the meaning of the word "faith", we find the following explanations: a reliance, a complete trust, a belief founded on authority, an unquestioning belief, a belief in divine truth, a firm belief in something of which there is no proof, complete confidence and loyalty.

However, in the Bible a very clear explanation of faith can be found in the book of Hebrews (11: 1):

> To have faith is to be sure of the things we hope for, to be certain of the things we cannot see.

My mother's approach to Christian faith is to unquestioningly accept the word of God and put her whole trust in Him. Trust is the beginning of faith, even though this emotion is often inexplicable. I have witnessed often enough that patients who were sceptical of the methods used in their treatment did not progress as well as those who completely trusted either the treatment or the practitioner.

I have seen that faith *can* work miracles, especially in cases where a patient has complete trust and, as a result of that trust, will fully co-operate. Then we can indeed experience striking and inexplicable improvement taking place in that patient's health.

Every now and then we hear or read about people who have such tremendous faith that they are able to perform miracles or superhuman feats. Of course we then wonder what the source of their faith is and in what context these superhuman performances were achieved.

In the Bible we read all about faith. We learn that Jesus Himself performed numerous miracles; in the New Testament about 20 per cent of the Gospels is dedicated to the healing miracles performed by Jesus. We also come to realise that Jesus was disappointed that the people followed Him in the hope of witnessing miracles being performed, whereas these miracles were only *signs* of the power of God in Him. He always pointed out that it was much more important to look for the Kingdom to come and when He spoke about that Kingdom, He mentioned that God would pour out His spirit in the coming of His Kingdom.

In the Old Testament book of Joel (2: 28-9) we receive an indication of God's intentions. The importance of becoming part of this future Kingdom will be so much greater than any visible or tangible healing miracles which took place on earth.

It is pointed out that inner healing would make men and women healthier spiritually, psychologically and physically. Therefore, a sincere worshipper of God should have the faith to believe that when there are problems in his or her life, and if it is God's will that the circumstances are altered, a miracle may take place.

Faith, however, is a very difficult and individual matter. This was also pointed out by Jesus to those disciples who were closest to Him. The reason that they were unable to perform the miracles He performed, was because of their unbelief or lack of faith. According to Jesus, if their faith was even the size of a mustard seed they could command mountains to move themselves and those mountains would be moved, because if they had faith nothing would be impossible, if God so willed it. Again, when His disciples asked Him how to increase their faith, He pointed out the importance of the Kingdom of God. Their dilemma shows how difficult it is to exercise faith, even for His disciples.

We have been given the wonderful story of Peter seeing his Master walking on the sea. When Jesus called out to him, Peter stepped out of the boat on to the water with complete faith. The faith in his subconscious mind was such that he walked across the water to his Master. When his conscious mind realised what he was doing, he began to sink. His Master saved him, but from this we learn what may be achieved by faith—the unconditional acceptance. In essence it could mean that subconsciously we are all capable of feats that we cannot perform when our logical mind takes over.

I remember my reaction as a child to the story of Peter walking on water. When we were told about this at school, I thought that it was worth trying out for myself. I went to the nearby river, stood on the banks and prayed very hard. When I stepped into the water, of course I sank. I had tried to put my faith to the test, but as I had been doubtful, I did not have the required faith in the first place. I never had the total confidence and the utter unawareness of danger as Peter did when he stepped out of the boat. Later I learned that only Peter was able to do this.

We also see in today's society that mankind is losing its image of spiritual potential. With all the understanding and knowledge—of both material and spiritual matters—we have acquired over the centuries, we have somehow lost a lot of our identity and spontaneous instinct. Many have even lost their spiritual task to explore the wonders of nature and have doubts about God, in some cases about His existence, and more so about His omnipotence.

How wonderful it would be if, through faith, we again could come to exist in harmony with ourselves and with God. Then we could take the first steps into reality and strive towards spiritual and mental healing.

A patient of mine had a complicated broken hip, which was almost beyond mending. However, she responded well to the various treatments she received at our clinic. When she was examined by her specialist in the hospital she was told that her improvement had been so startling and unexpected, that it was now time for her to learn to walk again.

Unfortunately she lacked the courage to walk. The physical injury had healed, but mentally she was still obsessed by a great fear and she had lost faith in her ability to ever walk again. She was now in need of healing of the mind.

Finally she did walk again, which was considered nothing short of a miracle by herself and by many of her friends. In order to walk, however, she had first to learn to believe that she was capable of walking. She had to have *faith* in order to be able to walk.

Prayer

Some time ago, a lady who had been a patient for many years came to tell me that she considered herself now completely cured and that she had experienced a miracle. This statement referred to the fact that, although over the years her condition had improved tremendously, there had still remained an ear and nose problem which we had failed to get under control.

She told me that one day she had decided to humble herself and go into her room to pray to God and beg Him for relief from this particular problem, if it was His will. To her mind she had never prayed like this before and as a result she had now completely overcome her affliction and felt like a new person.

In accordance with the advice Jesus gave us, to offer

44

prayers we should retire to a secluded place or a closed room where we may, without disturbance and interference, try to come in contact with God.

The lady concerned told me that she implicitly believed in God and that she had never prayed for anything for herself, but was completely encouraged now that she realised what a powerful experience prayer really was. The Bible teaches us that the prayer of a righteous person avails much.

Other people, too, have written about their understanding of prayer. Alfred Lord Tennyson said that more things are wrought by prayer than this world can dream of. Another of his sayings is that your prayer should be that you may have a sound mind in a sound body. One follows the other in my experience. The apostle Paul, on the other hand, says in his letter to the Ephesians that prayer should always be a supplication of the spirit.

Lots of people are disappointed when their prayers are not immediately answered. It is, however, God's will whether they be answered or not and we should always accept His decisions.

If God does not want healing for the body, neither medicine nor prayer will secure it. If it is not God's will and if it is not in our best interest, we have to realise that healing was not what God has in store for us. How wonderful if we could learn to accept God's will in full faith, as Paul learned to regard the thorn in his flesh which was not removed as God's will.

If we want to learn how to offer prayers we would do well to read some of the prayers in the book of Psalms. From some of the Scriptures we learn that certain prayers are fitting for specific occasions. Christ has given us the perfect guidelines for prayer, recorded in the Gospel of Matthew (6: 9-13), outlining the primary things that we should pray for. These have all been included in the Lord's Prayer.

Sickness befalls rich and poor alike and it is of great comfort to know that God can remove illness when He considers it appropriate. In the Bible we read of many miracles and wonders, in the Old as well as the New Testament, where total physical recovery of all types of illnesses and ailments took place. I frequently advise patients who are undergoing treatment that they should pray for the spiritual strength and awareness to open their mind to any physical treatment they are receiving.

In many cultures or religions some form or other of healing by prayer is claimed. However, Jesus has taught us exactly how to pray and also when God will answer our prayers. Even in the beginning God declared: "I am the Lord, the One who heals you," as is stated in the book of Exodus (15: 26).

Unfortunately there are many misunderstandings about prayer, which is such a valuable link between God and us. This particular subject is often taken out of context and it sometimes seems that we pressurise God to perform some healing or implore Him for signs, both of which go beyond the correct meaning of prayer.

If a person is "tuned in" with God and sends up his prayer, I am sure that an effectual, fervent prayer will bring His blessings. All prayers to Him who reigns, will for evermore bring a sovereign love.

Whilst God will give His love, we will share love with others. I enjoyed reading the book *Give Happiness a Chance* written by Phil Bosmans. The last chapter in this book bears the title: "Mankind, I love you". There he writes: "I believe in a miracle when in every house, in every street and in every city, people will say to their neighbours: 'My friends, I love you. Friends, mankind, I love you.'" To say this with or without words in itself, shows that prayer has taught us the One whom we should love first and not to offer selfish prayers, but prayers to help us and others.

I remember a particularly difficult time in my life when I prayed long and hard. I humbled myself completely before God and brought all my worries and anxieties to Him. While I was concentrating on my prayer to God, the words my aunt had taught us as children, suddenly came back to me: "God is always with you, whatever you do, and by His presence He will surprise you."

I have often experienced that fact and when I knew I lacked the necessary knowledge in treating very difficult cases, I have prayed to God for His help and guidance in the treatment of that patient. Sometimes I have experienced unexpected help, which goes beyond understanding, for which I give thanks to God.

There exists a close link between prayer and life, although frequently we regard them as unconnected incidences whilst they should be seen as inseparable. Often in their later years people grow to see prayer and life as a single entity. In order to offer an honest prayer one must be living in harmony with God, but the main requirement for prayer is that one is prepared to take the time for it. Think of the long hours Jesus spent in prayer with His Father. Reading about the miracles He performed should serve as a reminder of the importance of living in harmony with God. To come in close contact with God requires time. How much benefit we will receive from those quiet moments when we try to contact our Creator! We may then experience the wonder of receiving the restful peace of heart and mind that we seek.

Meditation

One evening, when I was locking up at about ten o'clock after having finished surgery, a young woman arrived pleading for help. I was tired, but nevertheless I realised that she indeed needed help desperately, as I could see from her face that something must have happened to badly upset her.

She told me that life had not always been too pleasant and that she had had her share of disappointments. She had followed the advice given to her by someone and had started to do simple yoga exercises in order to relax. She had seemed to benefit from these exercises, had continued further down the road of yoga and mental relaxation and became more interested in meditation. Eventually she had become snarled up by the occult. There, turning into her subconscious mind during intense meditation, she had lost all sense of reality, which caused such confusion that she became a psychiatric patient and had not been able to turn the clock back.

Meditation can constitute great danger if an incorrect approach is followed. Jesus has given us directions for correct meditation and the more we meditate upon things which belong to God and His great Kingdom, the more benefits we will receive out of meditation.

During the long talk we had, I tried to point this out to the young woman and guide her back to the right path. Eventually she found the balance which has made her the stronger person she is today. Her previous experiences in life could be used to her benefit if looked upon in a positive way.

I had a very special old friend, whom I greatly admired. Not only had he used his life to serve and help others less fortunate than himself, but he would also meditate at length on those aspects of life, which left him a very profound person.

When he was walking up the road one day, someone remarked to a friend of his: "He is getting old. Look, he is talking to himself." To this his friend immediately replied: "No, he is talking with God." And that was indeed the correct assumption, because I know that he discussed with God those things belonging to God's Kingdom and meditated on them. It was because of this that he was such a great person and able to display love to others and help them where needed.

In medicine it is considered that the correct medication results in appropriate relaxation and that minimal physical feelings exist under complete relaxation. This condition is obtainable from meditation also, where we learn to relax and thus create the opportunity for the body to heal itself.

I used to study my children when they were very young and their instinctive reactions fascinated me. Sometimes when both my wife and I were busy and they started to cry, we might not drop everything to attend to their wishes, but let them cry for a little while. We might give them a little toy and the crying might temporarily become a bit more subdued, but would continue. This was usually a cry out of boredom or to demand attention. The wail would most likely start up again shortly and abate when another toy was offered. However, when the crying was due to hunger and food was given, the baby would immediately stop crying. This crying was caused by a real need which had to be attended to.

I automatically associate meditation with prayer. We might pray and cry for help; we might meditate and ask for help—but our needs can only be fulfilled by Him who created us and who is aware of *all* our needs. Neither prayer nor meditation is therefore of use unless it is sincere and unselfish. If it is to meet our needs, like those babies, and our cry to God is for help, we will find that God will respond in His chosen way and our natural needs may be satisfied in whichever way He considers most appropriate.

It is extremely difficult to switch off one's mind. Our minds tend to be very agile; they will resort to all manner of tactics in order to keep the upper hand and they will not be easily tamed. If we learn to exercise a certain measure of self-control over our mind, we may experience better concentration and the ability to fix the mind on one thing at a time and direct our focus on our Creator.

Sometimes people maintain that meditation makes the mind vacant. It is impossible to render the mind vacant, as is also true of sleep. We only think that when we are asleep, everything is switched to neutral and our mind is vacant. This is not the case—the mind is active even in our sleep. Meditation is, however, a wonderful experience in which we can express to God all that is in our hearts and minds and ask Him to let us see ourselves as He sees us. Then we can learn to improve our lives in order to concentrate more on those things which belong to Him and His Kingdom and so become a better person. The same applies to nature, where everything is arranged according to an established order and beauty is to be found in everything.

Once we achieve that relationship with our Creator we will learn to discipline ourselves and train our minds on those things which are most important. We can then enjoy the peace and rest which settle within us. Then we can meditate according to the outlines given to us in the scriptures. As King David said in Psalm 19:

> Let the words of my mouth and the meditation of my heart be acceptable in Thy sight, O Lord.

I have studied the Zen masters with interest and I have seen how they are able to slow down the brain to 4-7 cycles, which is the Theta-wave level of subconsciousness, as opposed to the normal conscious level of 28 cycles (Beta-waves) per second. As a result, their metabolism is also slowed down and they are able to withstand pressures and stress under the most difficult circumstances. I have also seen them perform superhuman feats. This clearly shows that thought and mind control can slow down or speed up body processes, i.e. the heart races with excitement or slows down with relaxation.

Sometimes I point out to people who are looking for adventure that many things are *within* us. If one sincerely wishes to become a happier person, then look for that happiness which is within our reach, because God does supply us with most of the necessary ingredients for happiness, if only we are prepared to recognise them as such. If we approach our Divine Creator with that wish in our hearts, we will surely experience miracles if this is His will.

One of my previous colleagues summed up meditation as follows: "It is comparable to working as an alchemist. For years he hammers away at the same lump of metal. He melts it down and hammers it again for years and then re-forms it. This process may be repeated endlessly."

Our old ways of thinking have to be adapted and new habits need to be developed. It takes a long time for stress and tension to take root and before that is the case, we need to do something about it. Therefore, by working on ourselves in an attempt to become better persons, we will learn to relax through prayer and meditation. Tensions will disappear and both body and mind may relax.

When we keep working at it, we will experience that depressions decrease, more energy is gathered and we learn more about ourselves and those things when Godliness develops within us. Concentration sharpens, our body strengthens, we will experience a newer sensitivity to life and any difficulties or problems will appear more like experiences which are to be endured as a natural part of life. The result will be a deeper understanding of our own identity and the reason for our creation.

In the book of Kings we find the lovely story about the prophet Elijah. He was very depressed and in a dangerous position when he was called by an angel of God to stand on top of the mountain where God would speak to him. A tempestuous wind passed through the mountains, strong enough to shatter rocks, but God did not speak to him from that wind. Then there was an earthquake, but God was not in the earthquake. After the earthquake there was a fire, but God was not in the fire. Then there was a stillness, a soft whisper of a voice and Elijah could hear God's message. I am sure that Elijah's heart must have been filled with peace and love for God, because he immediately followed God's instructions and while being in God's service he was a blessing to many.

Faith, prayer and meditation still work like a miracle today and miracles beyond words or understanding are still performed, because these three aspects of spiritual life are related to our Creator. Yet, in our disobedience, do we realise how much we are missing by not taking advantage of a full understanding of them as revealed to us from the Scriptures?

4

Healing—A Miracle or an Extraordinary Event?

A VERY down-to-earth patient, who unfortunately suffers from the disabling disease of Multiple Sclerosis, has been attending our clinic for many years. A chemist by profession, this straightforward gentleman has been able to keep his problems in check due to his positive attitude.

He often tells me that he considers it a miracle how, between us, we have managed to keep him going all these years. Not knowing how to express his gratitude, he has always said that if he ever could do anything for me in return, I should not hesitate to ask him.

During a talk we had one day before I began to write this book, we decided that he would interview a number of people on my behalf and ask them the following questions:

Have you ever seen a miracle?
Have you ever heard of a miracle?
Have you personally experienced a miracle?

He was fascinated by the subject and looked forward to getting started with the project. On his next visit, to my surprise, he told me that he had put these questions to more than 200 people. Together with those who had been interviewed by me, this should cover a fair cross-section.

The topic of healing miracles had particularly seemed to stir the imagination of those he interviewed. However, on the whole, the response was very disappointing. The predominant answer to any of the questions was "No". Some non-believers said that they might have seen something of a miracle, but were not definite about it. This was also the general reaction from the Protestant section of those who were interviewed. Of the Roman Catholic section a few were more positive, while some of the more extreme religious groups had shown some inclination to be more receptive than most of those questioned. Unfortunately, when my "deputy" tried to trace these people, he ran into difficulties.

It just shows that claims of actually having experienced or witnessed a miracle must always be regarded very objectively. Looking at the present amount of publications on the subject of healing, we ought to realise that in order to make a correct judgement, superficial knowledge of a specific case is not enough. Unless we have background information we are not capable of judging fairly, as our first impressions are not always what they seem.

Although some people claim to possess healing powers, it is questionable how genuine these claims are, because we must appreciate that all healing indirectly comes from God. Even then, however, we have each to find an answer for ourselves to the following questions:

Is God capable of healing?
Does God always heal?
Does God ever heal?
What means of healing are used by God?

The Creator of all mankind is easily capable of healing, if this is His will. There are no limits to His power, but still we often see that God does allow suffering. He allowed His faithful servant Job to be afflicted by many forms of torment. He even allowed His true servant Paul to remain plagued by a thorn in the flesh and it is clearly stated that Paul was attacked by a messenger of Satan. We must, however, accept that God had His reasons for not healing either of these two men.

In His wisdom God does not always effect healing, nor does He always approve of healing. After all, as humans, we have no right to tell God what to do and we must learn to accept His decisions in faith.

I remember one occasion when my wife and I paid a sick-bed visit to a still youngish friend of ours. We, as well as the patient, were aware of the fact that this was our farewell visit, as there was very little time left for her. On our arrival we had barely been able to recognise her, as her body was totally emaciated as a result of cancer. When we expressed something of our admiration for the way she was coping with her suffering, she answered that she considered herself a rich person, because she knew what her Master had suffered for her. She was looking forward to a better life with Him than she had had here on earth.

When we came away from that visit, I said to my wife: "To think that an unbeliever, looking at such a person, could criticise the love of God. This person has given her life to the service of others and has ignored all normal rewards that life could bring. She has sacrificed her whole life out of love for others. Yet, at the end of her days of suffering, she feels a very rich person!" God allowed her to suffer, but she endured that suffering for the sake of His greater glory.

Some Christians look to God for healing, but are ignorant of the means which God might choose. They fail to see the very important principle that life is a gift from God and that it is His will to allow it to end. Admittedly, it is difficult to accept that He does allow suffering, even in His very dear ones, but in His almighty power His reasons for allowing this are hard to comprehend.

Once, on my arrival at a medical meeting, I accidentally entered the wrong hall. There, hundreds of people were assembled, listening to a speaker who was shouting and screaming to God to effect healing there and then on some of those unfortunates. He was trying to force the hand of God to show His healing powers at that particular moment.

The speaker even went so far as to encourage those people who were following the broadcast of this meeting at home to put their hands on the radio so that accordingly healing might take place.

Looking on, I saw no results. I was deeply ashamed to realise that the name of God was used for this public spectacle and was sad to see how gullible some people can be in their desperation. Of all those present, praying for relief, none came forward to claim response.

Some healing is allowed by God and if the individual prays and asks for healing, God in His wisdom will decide what action should be taken. This reminds me of reading in the Gospel of Saint John, Chapter 5, about the man who was waiting near the bath water of Bethesda. A crowd of sick people were waiting for the water to move, because every now and then an angel of the Lord went down into the pool and stirred up the water. The first sick person to go into the pool after the water was stirred up, was healed from whatever disease he or she was suffering.

This particular sick man, who was unable to walk, had been there for 38 years and was still waiting and hoping to be healed. When Jesus asked him: "Do you want to get well?" he answered: "Sir, I have no one there to put me into the pool when the water is stirred up. While I am still trying to get in, someone else always gets there first."

Here Jesus showed us clearly that healing comes from Him, because He said: "Get up, pick up your mat and walk."

Immediately the man stood up, picked up his mat and started walking.

After this physical healing, Jesus pointed out the infinitely greater importance of the healing of the mind or spirit in order to obtain eternal life.

As I have said, healing comes from Him who has the power to give and take life. No physician will claim that medicine does heal. They know too well that it is the life force within every individual which brings healing and that God can and does promote this because, as the Creator of life, He can restore and renew life. Whatever form healing may take, be it through natural healing, rest, nourishing foods, sleep, or any other remedy, healing ultimately only comes from God Himself and by obedience to the laws of nature, which are the laws of God.

Sickness and disease are never, under any circumstances, God's direct will and purpose. Why then is it that so many people are not healed? Why are so many people stricken with incurable diseases? There could be many reasons for this, such as bodily weakness, inherited tendencies or careless living habits. Human explanations are only guesses at the reasons behind the destiny decided for us by God. Hardness of the heart, mental disharmony, blood or hormonal imbalance may also be factors contributing to a lack of well-being and it must be left to God as to whether there will be a healing or not.

In my work over the years I have seen many examples of diseases and illnesses which often are the result of worry, stress, anger, jealousy, hatred and other harmful influences on the human body. Positive emotions, on the other hand—joy, faith, hope, love and confidence—can bring out healthier responses from the body.

A person may be analysed as a combination of mind, body and spirit. On finding true harmony with our Creator, and experiencing the love and peace of God, the happier attitude of our soul and mind will influence the body more positively.

Looking at the unhealthy attitude of many in the world today, where some seek to disturb even the balance of nature, we realise that there is no need to fear because, in spite of ourselves, God's power is still prevailing in nature, showing that He is continuing to be merciful towards us.

I would like to discuss several forms of healing, about which there are many misconceptions. Bearing in mind what I have written here so far, spiritual healing seems an appropriate starting point.

Spiritual healing

There is a certain danger in the amount of publicity which the subject of healing is getting nowadays. Spiritual healing seems to attract much, often unwarranted, attention and in some people it awakens an unhealthy interest in mystical rites.

Throughout the world I have witnessed examples of those methods which are referred to as spiritual healing and I have come to the conclusion that in many instances the name of Jesus is mentioned, despite the fact that the force of *evil* is used in those rituals. A patient's view of this matter is often encouraged by superstition and it is often the case that paganism is nowadays passed off as Christianity.

However, Christ made it perfectly clear that if we wanted to ask God for anything, we should go into isolation and while being alone with God, ask Him for His help. I myself have witnessed just what this can achieve. An elderly patient of mine desperately wanted to regain a greater degree of mobility, as he was barely able to shuffle along. He told me that he sincerely prayed to God to restore the use of his legs. Aided by this positive approach to the problem, he was granted his request, which in turn served to further increase his faith.

There is, too, the story that I mentioned earlier of Jesus raising Lazarus from the grave. When He was confronted by Lazarus' distraught sister, Mary, He felt compassion for her and ordered the mourners to remove the stone at the entrance to the cave where the body of Lazarus had been placed. He need not have asked to have the stone removed, as He could have done so himself with just one word. However, to show God's glory to the mourners He requested their co-operation. This may be interpreted as a sign that we have to show ourselves willing to make some effort.

Whenever he gives a lecture or seminar my good friend Dr Allen always points out that God will work *with* you, but He will not work *for* you. His help is not for the lazy ones. We have to take an active part in working with God towards the things we ask Him to do.

Mankind has drifted far away from the energies which are available in the Kingdom of God. The contact between man and the Kingdom of Heaven has moved into the background because of the pressures of society today. That contact is the ultimate form of healing for mind, body and spirit. Instead of striving towards it, we have adopted different priorities into our lives.

In making claims on the subject of healing, one has to be extremely careful, because it all depends on whether long-term improvement or healing has been affected.

I have frequently had the opportunity to watch spiritual healers at work. It is really not terribly difficult to induce a kind of euphoric condition while working on a person. This phenomenon could be explained as stimulation of that person's own natural energies, yet the result is often regarded as a miracle. Whether the improvement is long-standing is, however, more to the point in deciding if we are dealing with a miracle.

One particular lady had been having treatment at our clinic for quite some time for Multiple Sclerosis. Her condition seemed reasonably stable, but we certainly had not made any drastic progress, despite the fact that we had both worked very hard at it.

What did bring about a change in her condition, however, was the fact that she had set her wedding date. She said that without doubt it would be the happiest day of her life if she were able to walk up the aisle by herself.

Looking at her, this seemed absolutely impossible, but she actually managed to do just that. She was ecstatic and the wedding guests, who witnessed the fact, were deeply impressed. I only wished that it had lasted, but unfortunately it did not. She had experienced what could best be described as a euphoric climax and when the euphoria wore off, the effects also disappeared.

Thinking of this patient, I am also reminded of a young gentleman who regularly visits the clinic. Every time I see him leave after treatment, he seems full of the joys of life and people think that I have worked a miracle on him. He is absolutely buoyant compared to the way he looks when he arrives. What those people don't realise is that this euphoria does not last—it is like a self-induced drug. On every visit he is elated and feels that things are on the mend, but when his optimism fades he physically deteriorates again.

Some of the people I have interviewed on the subject did claim to have experienced a miracle. When, however, it came to the crunch of the matter, they were vague about how and when it occurred. True spiritual healing is a matter of finding harmony within oneself and with our Creator. If a natural relationship has been established between God and ourselves, a miracle *has* occurred. Only then can God give spiritual healing, when we are mentally, bodily and spiritually an integral part of His Creation.

Unfortunately, I have been disappointed too often by so-called spiritual healers, whose main aim seems to be to collect their rewards here on earth. They amass their earthly gains by profiting from ailing people. Those misguided unfortunate people are promised that with the spiritual help they are being given, healing might be effected.

However, in the book of Revelations (16: 14), we are told to be aware of spirits or demons that perform miracles. It almost looks, in today's society, as if the world is being swept with evil spirits. Let us remember that spiritual healing need not endanger mankind, but that health can only be maintained where perfect harmony between soul, mind and body exists.

The laying-on of hands

Some time ago I was present at the graduation ceremony of some young medical practitioners. The speech at this ceremony was given by the Vice-President of the Red Cross, Dame Kathleen Raven. This lady has spent her life in an effort to ease suffering and alleviate the conditions which are the cause of suffering and disease. She has been heavily involved in world-wide nursing management and certainly impressed me with her speech.

She said that the greatest gifts of nurses and practitioners were their hands. Hands can bring such comfort to ailing persons. They may be used to convey the feelings of friendship and understanding.

From infancy we are trained to express our thoughts and purpose of mind—and our hands are the tools of the mind. They may be used to convey thoughts into action. Look at the way a baby uses its hands long before it displays any other signs of awareness or recognition. The primitive native, with fewer words in his vocabulary, depends on his hands to express his thoughts. A hand may also lift those who have stumbled or fallen and good wishes may be expressed by a handshake.

Hands have been used at the most important ceremonials since the dawn of civilisation. They may serve symbolically in actions to which we have learned to respond: deaf and dumb people are able to communicate with their hands and blind persons use their hands for reading.

My dear friend, Dr Allan, says it so well in his book *Body Energy Techniques*, where he uses the expression that the hand of God, which has reached out to us in pity, will help us through all experiences of life and that God's healing power is the only healer of man's ills. It is true that the hand of God can guide the hands of the practitioners. Not by using flattering language in an attempt at persuasion, not by bribery, cajoling, or threats will the hand of God be forced to heal.

God's gift of healing is found in nature and is available to everyone who adheres to the laws of nature. These laws are simple. Everyone who wants to make use of His great gifts to mankind can help himself by programming the mind with a positive outlook.

The mind acting, is the mind thinking. The result of thinking is thoughts and of the mind's action is the mind's thoughts. All thoughts, whether conscious or unconscious, are expressed, but many of them are expressed only in the organism of the thinker. The mind needs no words to command the hands.

The right hand has a positive palm and the back of the hand is negative; the left hand has a negative palm, while the back of the hand is positive. When illness strikes, these energies must be balanced.

Even thousands of years ago the ancient Chinese found that much may be achieved if the negative and positive energy in certain parts of the body can be brought into harmony and hands were used the right way. They also knew that in the abdominal area, around the navel, there are reflex areas where pain can be relieved by using the energy from one's hands to release and unwind the stress of pain. In that particular area we find the abbreviations of many organs, any of which could be the cause of developing pains.

In this area are the reflexes of the heart, gall-bladder, stomach, spleen, lungs, kidneys, liver, small intestines, colon and bladder. Here our hands come into their own and can be of so much use and thus here it is that the laying-on of hands becomes a practical means to obtaining fast relief from pain.

Some simple guidelines for these methods are as follows:

Fever	Cool body:	Left hand on back of head, right hand on solar plexus.
	Warm body:	Right hand on back of head, left hand on solar plexus.
Tiredness		Right hand in hollow of neck, left hand on adrenals.
Pneumonia		Left hand on back of head, right hand on solar plexus.
Nerves		Right hand on back of head, left hand on solar plexus.

Disease	Left hand on back of head, right hand on pain.
Influenza	Left hand on back of head, right hand on solar plexus.
Glands	Left hand on left side of head, right hand on forehead.
Healing	Left hand behind head, right hand on forehead.

I taught an old lady some of these simple methods. She had suffered much pain over the years as a result of shingles. In desperation she had visited spiritual healers, faith healers as well as those who practise the laying-on of hands, but none of them had been able to produce the required effect. Then I taught her that the energy she needed was in herself. In the end it was the harmonisation of her own energy that gave her the relief from pain for which she had been searching for so long.

It is wonderful to know when a balanced energy between us and the universe is established, and to realise how this energy may be applied when there is disharmony in the body. There is no doubt about the fact that these energies exist and can be applied for the purpose of healing. Every organ, tissue, muscle or bone is in direct or indirect contact with the surface area of the human body.

These facts are recognised by most scientists nowadays. It is quite a logical process to understand the workings of the sympathetic and para-sympathetic nerves, which supply and serve the body. With strong energy, contact may be made which will change an adverse situation. This is often the case where healing has been affected by the laying-on of hands.

In an earlier book on *Stress and Nervous Disorders*, I have given instructions on how this energy can be increased and how existing energy can be influenced by means of using the Hara breathing method in the navel area, which is the abdominal brain. This serves not only to energise the lymph and bloodcells, but also the body-tissue cells.

God in His wisdom used soil from which He moulded the shape of man in order to make him into a living being. He breathed the breath of life into his nostrils. Without energy man cannot exist and it is essential to learn to balance positive and negative energy.

Disease is a state of imbalance. Life is energy and all energy is vibration. By this gentle stimulation of the cells, one can influence life's energy to a tremendous extent. As a result of these factors I conclude that many miracles, or events that are referred to as miracles, are in fact some form of emotional response.

Our body is composed of myriads of cells, each with its own potential and vibration. Nothing rests—everything vibrates at a set frequency to achieve harmony. This motion is necessary and is of an electrical nature. It possesses a frequency which is essential to organic existence. Therefore disease is not an entity to be expelled from the body, but a dynamic error in the life forces. The imbalance in the vital functions can be corrected by the root co-operative power within the living cells.

These wise words are quoted from the foreword of Dr Allan's book on energy techniques.

> A hand for genuine comfort can be the only true meaning of healing by the laying-on of hands and this should never be used for the exploitation of unfortunate people for commercial gain.

Knifeless surgery

This is a psychic form of surgery, where operations are performed with bare hands which are painless and leave no scars.

Whenever we read descriptions of these practices, we are sceptical as to how this is possible. I had better inform you immediately that I have personally been a witness to such a demonstration and that it was unbelievable. With astonishment I witnessed these knifeless operations, where the patient indeed felt no pain, hardly any blood was spilt and no scar was left.

In some parts of the world (most notably in the Philippine Islands) these healing methods are performed regularly. Sometimes, however, fraudulent practices or self-delusion are suspected, although certain phenomena occur which cannot be explained in any way.

The persons who perform these knifeless operations are looked upon as wonder healers. Some kind of supernatural power seems to be at work here, but when we look at it objectively it is questionable where these powers stem from.

In the Philippines, where the largest proportion of the population are Roman Catholic, these extraordinary healings are done without permission from the Roman Catholic Church. They are performed by both Roman Catholics and non-Catholics in the name of Jesus Christ. Some claim that they are scientists, while others claim to possess supernatural God given powers, with which nature has endowed them. As an investigator, looking upon this with an open mind, one has to draw one's own conclusions.

Is a phenomenon like this possible? Can we reasonably accept these healings with an open-minded attitude as a medical feat, or are we dealing with hallucinations, imagination, hypnotic influences or clever tricks from magicians? One just has to decide for oneself if ever given the opportunity to witness one of these operations.

It appals me, however, that certain operations are performed in the name of the Holy Spirit, while it is more likely that the powers displayed are those of the devil. Some of these wonder healers profess to work out of a firm belief in God and a genuine attitude towards Him, while others will admit only to believing in the existence of a certain protector. This aspect certainly deserves careful consideration before deciding how to appraise these operations.

On occasions where no results are obtained, the patient is

sometimes blamed for being too sinful or for not having studied the Bible sufficiently. Psychic surgery too often focuses on religion or on so-called "God-power" or a spirit and yet is sometimes used for selfish benefits and ulterior motives.

To evaluate exactly what so-called psychic surgeons or healers achieve is an almost impossible task. There are many reports available, presenting a diversity of opinions, but none of these leaves us in any doubt that strange occurrences do take place.

Unfortunately, lots of money is to be made and therefore many claim to have the gift of divine healing. The bystander must finally judge for himself what his position is to be: will he maintain a sceptical attitude, will he be convinced and believe, or will he hover somewhere in between?

There is no doubt that we are dealing here with a very controversial subject and in order to form a true picture we first need the answers to many questions.

In the Bible we are given some very worthwhile advice in 1 John (4: 1):

> Do not believe all who claim to have the Spirit, but test them to find out if the Spirit they have comes from God. For many false prophets have gone out everywhere.

With this advice in mind, let each individual, according to his beliefs and principles, make his own judgement.

Healing with love

I was always intrigued whenever I heard my grandmother relate the story about an early girlfriend of hers, who had fallen in love and, when rejected, had eventually died of a broken heart. When the relationship was broken, she had started to suffer from some of the most extraordinary illnesses and imaginary diseases, which no doctor was able to treat.

An older doctor, after having thoroughly studied her

symptoms, eventually diagnosed that she was dying of a broken heart. This is indeed what happened. Although relatives and friends had tried to help her, she never was able to forget her love.

This story goes to show how strong and powerful an emotion love is and therefore it need not come as a surprise that love is a power to be reckoned with in healing.

Parents can often influence and accelerate the recovery of their children with that little bit of extra love, to which the child perhaps will be extra sensitive when ailing. On the other hand, we regularly witness a negative approach in people who are subjected to illness or disease—and this could well stem from a lack of love.

We realise the power of love when observing the relationship between mother and child, which can produce such positive action in the lives of both of them. I heard a particularly poignant example of this from my eldest daughter, who works as a district midwife in London. She told me recently that she had been asked to deliver a baby in a harem. The father of the baby she was to deliver lived with his harem of about 100 wives in London. After delivering the baby, who turned out to be a healthy boy, she noticed tears in the mother's eyes, not from happiness but from distress. She actually looked rather ill and when my daughter asked her if she was not happy with her child, she was told that the baby had to be handed over to another of the sheik's wives, who held a more important position in the harem.

My daughter, with her deep understanding and appreciation of maternal love, assured the mother that she would be able to have another baby, which, as was the custom in the harem, she would then be able to call her own.

In this case, love was the initial cause of the distress, because the mother was forced to part with her baby, but then she found consolation in the love and understanding offered to her by my daughter. Love can be the reason of happiness as well as unhappiness, which proves that it is an extremely powerful emotion.

Jesus healed so many with His compassionate love and still continues to do so today. All through history we come across examples where healing through love has taken place, yet in today's often uncaring, harassed and pressurised society, compassion is often underrated or, worse, considered to be misplaced. Let us not forget how many people in their loneliness are thirsting for love. It is no exaggeration to say that it sometimes may be regarded as a lifesaver.

When Captain James Cook dropped anchor off the coast of Kauai on 19 January 1778, he broke the isolation of the Hawaiian Islands from the rest of the world. The Hawaiians were neither corrupt nor ignorant, but showed themselves as an extremely loving people. From the example they set us, we were given an insight into the healing which can be affected through true love for one another.

The creed of the Kahunas is: "Ye shall know them by their fruits," i.e. positive thoughts can influence and/or alter any earthly thoughts. Their belief, which is fundamentally based on reality, appeals to me. They say that you create your own reality by your principles, in order that you may be of help to others.

Their teachings maintain that every human being is responsible for his or her own actions and for the results of those actions. In other words: if you commit violence—you will meet with violence; if you give love—you will be loved in return.

The Kahunas believe that a patient may express negative thoughts and that treatment by so-called faith healers, which is adapted to different identities, could result in worse problems. True healing is based on belief and only when that belief is present will a cure be effectively accomplished.

Manipulation is often practised by these people, which harmonises the energy in the human body. Accordingly they believe that the result lies in what has gone before. They admire and practise brotherly love, which includes the sharing of joy and, as they recognise God in everything, they practise joy, happiness and health in their belief that their lives will be renewed.

The reader must judge this philosophy for himself, but I have studied many people, especially in the so-called "uncivilised" parts of the world, where I could not fail to notice their harmony with God. This harmony encourages a caring and loving attitude and by giving love one would receive love in return. There is no harm in occasionally looking into ourselves to see where we have withheld love, or loved ourselves more than others. If we find that we have done so, we will have let someone else down, someone who trusted us. This would also be a reflection of the fact that we have not learned, or most certainly do not practise, the most important lesson Jesus taught us in the New Testament, namely the lesson of love.

This lesson is to be found in Saint John (13: 34):

> And now I give you a new commandment. Love one another. As I have loved you, so you must love one another.

5

The Miraculous Water of Lourdes

IT IS QUITE a few years since I was invited to lecture at an international conference in Bienne, Switzerland, on my methods of treatment for Multiple Sclerosis. Following an afternoon lecture on this subject, I returned to my hotel, where I had an unexpected visitor—Professor Karl Asai from Japan.

We talked till deep into the night about our mutual interest in natural medicine and he told me a most surprising story about a first-hand experience he had undergone in Lourdes. He stated that he was neither a philosopher nor devoutly religious, but was primarily a researcher of natural sciences.

Because of the research work he had been involved in, he wanted to discuss some of his findings with me, which he felt might be incorporated in the treatment of Multiple Sclerosis. He invited me to partake in a research programme as to the benefits of using the mineral Germanium, also known under atomic number 32.

He told me that he recognised laws of a kind incomprehensible to man and originating from nature. With a great deal of courage he had started to make some facts public after having conducted extensive research. All this had begun after he was diagnosed as suffering from a malignant tumour in the throat for which surgical removal would be extremely difficult. He was then persuaded to go to Lourdes to try and find help there.

Around that time he had read some articles written by Alexis Carrell entitled "Journey to Lourdes" and "Man the Unknown", as well as another article in *Newsweek*. It was this last article that particularly attracted his attention.

The *Newsweek* article was about a three-year-old girl who was dying of cancer. One of her kidneys had been removed, but the cancer had spread to the cranial bone. She had become emaciated, her hair had fallen out and her skin had turned yellow. Her whole system was affected by cancer and the doctors had given her up as a hopeless case. The surgeon at the Sick Children's Hospital in Glasgow, Scotland, recalled that the blastoma had spread everywhere. The case had gone beyond surgery and the little girl displayed all the signs of impending death.

As a last resort, the child's desperate mother, being a Roman Catholic, decided to take her daughter to the shrine of Our Lady of Lourdes. There the semi-conscious little girl was dipped in the sacred water. The girl, however, was obviously in pain and the pilgrimage was cut short as her mother wanted to get back to Scotland so that she could die at home.

During the first two days after their return the Scottish doctors watched the child slip further towards her death. Then, on the morning of the third day, she sat up in bed and asked for an orange. She seemed to eat this with enjoyment and almost overnight her condition started to improve. Some time later the tumour disappeared and she once again became a healthy girl.

This story created a major sensation in the medical circles in Scotland and the fame of the miraculous water of Lourdes spread widely. The girl's doctor, a Protestant, insisted that the word "miracle" was indeed suitable for this occasion.

Professor Asai told me that after reading these articles and under pressure from family and friends, he went to Lourdes himself. He decided to drink as much as possible from the water of Lourdes in order to give himself a good chance.

After he had been there for a while he realised that a change had taken place, that the tumour in his throat had begun to shrink, and he grew very enthusiastic. But, as he was not a zealously religious person, he could not accept that this particular incident was due to a purely religious factor. After a lot of thought he came to the conclusion that it must be due to something extraordinary in the water of Lourdes, which he then determined to investigate. He transported a quantity of the water to Japan for research and found that it contained the mineral Germanium.

As he was already aware that Germanium develops additional oxygen in the bloodstream, he immediately realised the medical implications of his findings. He wondered if this was the secret of the miraculous water of Lourdes, which over many years has been claimed to have caused dramatic miraculous cures.

Professor Asai began a long period of research with these specific water samples. He also found a source of similar water in a retreat in Japan itself, where it had also been claimed that miracles have taken place. These, too, had been accredited to a religious influence. Both these waters contained so much of the mineral Germanium that he was struck with the idea of looking into the possibility of making organic Germanium, synthesized and soluble in water.

When Germanium is dissolved in water the solution should remain clear, no matter how long it has been preserved. This solution has demonstrated miraculous effects on various diseases, which previously had been extremely difficult to cure. It is particularly beneficial to patients suffering from tumours. When taken internally it produces a curative effect similar to that which had first drawn the attention of Alexis Carrell.

As part of his research on the water of Lourdes Professor Asai made an atomic absorption analysis of it. As anticipated, he was able to confirm the existence of nearly 30 parts per million of Germanium in a solution of 10% concentration.

He felt that he had discovered a possible scientific explanation for some of the miracles: perhaps they were potentially brought about by Germanium atoms. The latent power in the Germanium atoms acted as a catalyst on those suffering from tumours, allowing the body to absorb the malignancy.

Since organic Germanium compound supplies oxygen to the body cells, one will feel less tired, even though the actual sleeping time might have been cut short. Organic Germanium compound is discharged from the body in about 20 to 30 hours once it has coursed through the body, and no known side-effects are produced. This was another reason for Professor Asai to investigate the possibilities this mineral created in greater depth. Today, the Asai Institute on Research of Organic Germanium is well known throughout the world. Professor Asai succeeded, before he died, in encapsulating Germanium.

I was lucky enough to work together with Professor Asai for quite some time before he died of old age. We took tests on different types of patient. The effects of organic Germanium has been a blessing for many of my patients and I recall specifically some of the Multiple Sclerosis patients on this programme, who showed tremendous response.

I think back to a letter I received, written by the mother of a six-year-old child who was dying of a brain tumour. The letter stated that since her child had started taking organic Germanium capsules, the situation had totally changed. Although the child was only six years old, she suffered several epileptic fits daily and was not able to do anything for herself. The organic Germanium stopped the epileptic fits and in time she was even able to ride her little bicycle. A dramatic change indeed—due to Germanium—which has been experienced by other patients, who generally have responded well.

I discussed the miracle of Lourdes with Professor Asai and stressed that he should not overlook the fact that many people experienced healing out of faith. We debated whether it might not be the case that a combination of natural healing properties in the water, together with a sincere faith, were responsible for some of the miracles which have taken place in Lourdes. He agreed that faith is always a great help, but he felt that the miracles were to a larger extent accreditable to the wonderful physical properties which the water of Lourdes contains. Through publications on the subject, people have been made aware that Lourdes water may be of great benefit and so their expectations are raised and their hope and faith strengthened.

Doctors in Lourdes keep a careful register of any miraculous results reported by visitors to the shrine. I have spoken to many people who have visited Lourdes and in my opinion it is their positive attitude and strong desire to get better which has been their biggest asset in obtaining relief or the cure they set out for. However, there is no doubt in my mind that this water contains Germanium in such rich quantities that it must be of great help for ailing people. A positive attitude rarely fails to produce some results.

I recently heard from a lady in Aberdeen who has monitored the healing processes in Lourdes for a long time. She wrote to me about a young soldier who was a non-believer. During an accident he was seriously injured and his hip had nearly crumbled away.

X-rays were taken to the group of doctors at Lourdes who investigate any claims of cures or progress and they clearly showed the irreparable damage to the young man's hip bone. He drank the water of Lourdes and had several baths in the water and started to notice signs of improvement. After a period of time new X-rays indicated considerable signs of improvement. It seemed almost as if the young man had undergone a hip replacement operation. It was indeed an inexplicable improvement and the delighted young man could testify from his own experience to the miraculous healing powers of the water of Lourdes.

It is, however, said that the percentage of actual cures at

Lourdes is low—a higher percentage of sick people who visit Lourdes leave there uncured. From these figures we realise that miracles or unexpected changes in the human body do not always happen at the time when we want them to—and sometimes they never will.

Claims of healing miracles are always difficult to evaluate as we all visualise certain happenings in a different light. Lourdes, there is no doubt, does constitute for many people a great *spiritual* experience. The healing properties of Germanium will assist, but certainly will not always provide a cure. The cures differ to a large extent, as to the degree that supernatural intervention by God is demonstrated. Some cures are visibly of supernatural origin, but sometimes God chooses to work in a less obvious manner and will provide healing through natural causes.

One thing, however, is clear: through close inter-relationship between our physical and our spiritual health, sickness might be overcome. The root of the problem may be removed through faith and prayer.

Professor Asai felt more positive about the procedure and concluded that the miracles ascribed to the water of Lourdes were due principally to the Germanium it contained. The concept became clear to him, that with a positive attitude coupled with the healing properties of Germanium, a cure could be obtained.

The findings of his research in Germanium have been a blessing to many people. In his book *Organic Germanium—A Medical Godsend* Professor Asai gives much scientific information about Germanium, which is present in such high quantities in the water of Lourdes.

He believed that a certain cycle of phenomena in nature may be considered as a kind of transmigration. Metallic elements in the soil are absorbed by plants, contributing towards the growth of these plants, while animals take metallic elements into their bodies by eating these plants. Within the body, inorganic metallic elements are turned into organic matter and these elements are eventually returned to the soil through discharge or death. It is conceivable that certain elements, including Germanium, contribute to the growth of life following the orbit of transmigration in nature. If we introduce this orbit of transmigration of Germanium into our living system, we can avoid the constant contraction of serious diseases such as cancer and maintain health in conformity with the laws of nature.

Such was his train of thought. It is true that Germanium is indispendable to transistors and it is a useful element in the forefront of the electronics industry. It does play an important role in the maintenance of health, hence the reason that when we find Germanium in certain plants and flowers, i.e. mushrooms, garlic and ginseng to name but a few, it is to our benefit that we eat these particular Germanium-rich products.

Professor Asai has debated the properties of Germanium with many people. He was convinced that Germanium, as a four-dimensional substance, directly connected with life, is essential for man's existence.

In my dealings with patients I have often been able to witness the beneficial effects of this mineral. Since that unexpected meeting in Switzerland with the Professor, I have been grateful for the opportunity of doing some research work with him and the letters of gratitude I have received from patients have made it very worth while.

Where patients had seemingly been beyond help, Germanium has displayed its wonderful characteristics. For example, the suffering of a cancer patient in possibly the last hours of his life may be eased by Germanium. That in itself is a great miracle for those who are in pain or struggling with the experience of life drawing to an end on this earth.

6

The Miracle of Nature

IT ALWAYS AMAZES me to see how many self-healing miracles nature is capable of performing. When we look into the beauty of nature, apparent everywhere in the world, we may be surprised at the enormous powers which Creation holds and should regard them with the greatest respect. To be able to witness those healing powers with which nature has provided us, is in itself a miracle.

How is it possible that mankind has so abused this wonderful Creation? While writing this chapter I am forced, due to recent events, to think of the great threat of nuclear radioactivity. We seem to be able to choose to use these powers of nature for our destruction as well as for our benefit. Man, with his great instinct for science, is capable of destroying the health of mankind in his thirst for power and ambition.

I remember flying quite low over Windscale one day and I was able to see what man had created there in order to obtain nuclear energy. How fearful it looked! Despite its doubtful benefits, we have taken on our shoulder a great irresponsibility towards future generations. What are we going to do with all that waste material? Why are we destroying so much of nature and its beauty?

Due to a fire at Windscale in October 1957 two aluminium cylinders were damaged in the plutonium factory. The accident was kept secret for 24 hours and it is likely that it would have remained a secret but for a difference of opinion within the management team. The news leaked eventually and then messages of warning were sent out.

It was decided to instruct farmers in an area of approximately 500 miles not to use their land for agricultural purposes and about 600,000 pints of milk were disposed of because of the risk of radiation. As the recent experience of Chernobyl has shown us, the earth's atmosphere can be contaminated very quickly.

Let us consider the generations to come and look specifically at newly born babies. They are themselves a miracle. When we look at these small human beings, should not our aim be to provide them with the best possible natural surroundings? It is our responsibility that these innocent little ones should not have to cope with a society which has destroyed much of the natural beauty and goodness with which the world was endowed.

Let us remember, too, that nature's healing powers will perform the most wonderful miracles, to which no human hand can lay claim. Even where many scientific methods have failed, nature may claim victory.

A few weeks ago I received a visit from a young couple, who had last consulted me five years previously. Then, they had told me that as they were happily married they would love to have a child, but the doctors and specialists had informed them that this was not possible. The sperm count of the man was inadequate and the woman had suffered endometriosis and as such it was hardly possible that between them they would be able to produce a baby.

They had come to ask me for advice the second time round, as not too long after having consulted me the first time, and having followed some simple guidelines based on nature, the woman had become pregnant and given birth to a healthy baby boy. The specialist's reaction had been: "A miracle!" They were now back to see me as they hoped to increase their family. Let this be a lesson to us not stray too far from nature and never to underestimate it.

With our hectic lifestyle nowadays it is often difficult to come into harmony with nature. However, if that stage has been reached, and we learn to appreciate the importance of living in such harmony, then this will be like experiencing a miracle.

We abuse our bodies in so many ways, but is nature not our best friend? It is surely proven to us when we consider the healing process within a scar. We can witness how quickly the scab drops off and fades. That is the miracle of nature at work.

The other day I again saw one of my patients, whom I knew suffered some rather unusual problems. Having talked them through with her previously, I had given her some sensible advice regarding a natural wholesome diet and had prescribed some natural medicine, but she still kept feeling unwell. She had begged her doctors over and over again for help, but they had told her that after her operation everything was in order.

One morning she heard a clatter when going to the toilet and it appeared that nature had been kind to her and had cleared her system of an operation-clip, which the surgeon had overlooked during the operation. It had found its own way out. To be rid of this foreign body, which had caused her a lot of discomfort, was all that was needed for a drastic improvement in her condition. I was happy that I had advised her to continue with a healthy diet, so that nature would be able to do its job and that at one point, when she was utterly depressed and in tears, I had reminded her of the words of Robert the Bruce: "If at first you don't succeed, try, try again."

After this foreign body had dislodged itself and left her system, she was certainly repaid for her patience and she felt so much better.

There are many ways open to us, but we should not interfere with nature, nor take too many chances. How often do we use the expression: "Let nature take its course." If we place our trust in that acceptance, nature will very often surprise us. It will take care of us like a mother does of her children.

If we look slightly deeper into the subject we cannot get away from the old phrase: *Vis Medicatrix Naturae*—the power of nature has since ancient times been acclaimed as the power that heals. It was due to that power that medicine has made such progress in the medieval centuries. It is no wonder that still today the aim of a good naturopath should be to consider nature as the healer of all ills.

The other Satuday morning I went very early to the Post Office and was surprised to see how much filth and rubbish was left on our famous golf courses in Troon. I breathed in the fresh air and looked out over the sea and saw all its beauty. Everything seemed fresh and clean and the overnight cleansing effect was impressive. Then I thought of the ways in which we attack our bodies and of the simple methods available to us to detoxify our bodies. Here nature displays its miraculous properties.

A favourite expression comes to mind, which was used by Arnold Priesnitz, who lived from 1823 to 1906: "Water is good, air is better and sun is best." This now obvious remark was startling in those days and it inspired many of his contemporaries. A good naturopath will always look at the clinical observations of the healing process in which the body throws off its toxic accumulation by way of an acute crisis. Nature does not err; it will never make a mistake.

Both my grandmother and her mother were faithful followers of natural healing methods and practised the Kneipp cures. Basically, these cures were a combination of hydrotherapy, sunshine, exercise and a wholesome diet. These European nature cures, as advocated by Father Sebastian Kneipp, profoundly and permanently influenced the thinking of many and have consequently been adopted in many countries.

It is rightly so that the Kneipp ideas are accepted as the

birth of naturopathy, whereby it was considered that the practice should embrace all known means of natural therapeutics including diet, herbal methods, homoeopathy, exercises and individual counselling.

Diseases will alter physiology and pathology and when man fails to live in accord with natural and biological laws, or actually violates these, we will receive warnings. Today, man is not able to retreat into the ideal pollution-free Garden of Eden and therefore we should use the lesson of nature and build up our immune system. This will help us to withstand the attacks on the necessary energies for life, i.e. water, food and air.

In my time I have seen many "miracles" occur for which diet was largely responsible. Our diet should always be as natural and pure as possible. In some clinics I have visited I have seen cancer patients who had reached a progressive stage of the disease return eventually to normal health after following a healthy dietary regime and a natural lifestyle.

I quote here from a letter I received from a patient:

At the beginning of 1978, aged 53, I went to see my doctor (whom I had not visited for ten years) because of increasing fatigue, along with other indications that all was not well with me.

He immediately decided to give me a thorough examination, which he carried out six weeks later, at the conclusion of which he stated that I had fibroids and would need to see a specialist. Another six weeks later, I visited the gynaecologist, who also gave me an external and internal examination, recording that there was an incomplete emptying of the bladder due to a urine infection, but no disease. I was prescribed more tablets, but given no explanation of the severe pain in my left side.

Six months after this, I had the first of a number of small lumps with a spot like a boil coming up on various parts of my body. A skin specialist treated me with ointment.

In the late autumn of 1979, I began bleeding profusely from

my bladder, and the subsequent X-rays revealed a tumour within my bladder.

For almost two years, my strength had been continually ebbing away, so that I was forced to rest a great deal, and the feeling of illness prevailed. I lost three stone.

My doctor explained to me that unless I had, at least, my bladder removed at once and replaced, I would only live for a short while. Because of a personal aversion towards the description of my future bodily state following the surgeon's major operation, I withdrew, since I felt unable to learn to live with such a thing. Having watched my mother suffer, endure two operations and die of malignant cancer ten years previously, did nothing to inspire faith in this kind of remedy.

Through friends I heard of Jan de Vries, and flew to Scotland, since I was too weak to travel by road. His kindly manner gave me confidence, and his careful attention and concentration made me hopeful. I began his treatment and followed the special diet, as well as taking the additional natural medicine he recommended.

Very gradually I stopped going downhill and levelled out. Imperceptibly at first, but definitely, I began to feel a little less ill. Slowly the bleeding stopped altogether and I started to put on weight and get some colour into my face. After one year I commenced taking very short walks, and now walk for an hour each day.

Everything that Jan de Vries told me to do I carried out to the letter, as one cannot play around with cancer. It is a constant fight. He said to get plenty of fresh air, and this I did, along with deep breathing daily. His suggestion to go into the sea I also managed.

I ate only organically grown food for two years, despite the monotony caused by the difficulty in obtaining any variety, especially during winter-time, and also drank quantities of beetroot-juice, as instructed by Jan de Vries.

I certainly do testify to the benefit I have received from this safe method, since I can now accomplish most tasks and live a normal life, with a complete cessation of pain.

I thank my Creator and all those who have helped me in so many ways. It is good to be alive.

Not only has the condition obviously been arrested, but the growth appears to be shrinking, as there is much less discomfort, more room in my bladder and less movement, too, which I can feel in certain positions. My liver, which was also affected, gives me practically no trouble now, so a return to excellent health seems to be in sight.

Sometimes I can hardly believe it has all happened.

The writer of that letter has surely understood that nature, if we adhere to its laws, discloses our Creator to us and also that a true philosophy of nature deepens and strengthens that bond. The influence of nature is powerful, elevating and suggestive, and often so mysterious that in itself it is a miracle when man succeeds to live in harmony with Creation.

No man can ever behold the full beauty of nature. In the book of Ecclesiastes (3: 11) we find a peculiar passage where it is said that God has made everything beautiful in its time; also He has put eternity into man's mind, yet so that he cannot find out what God has done from the beginning to the end.

The more we learn to communicate with nature the more benefits we will receive when following its commands. By exercising in the fresh air we may calm the storms of life which often disturb our peace and tranquillity. If we do not learn to recognise and appreciate the powers of nature, we will never be able to demonstrate the healing practices with which nature is endowed.

Science is invaluable, but do not ask a scientist to explain how or why a blade of grass grows. It is not possible to explain this because we have not discovered the secret of the universe. We must accept the existence of that great power which provides life and growth, and it remains for everybody to direct this power to their chosen purposes.

When God created earth He made us the promise to supply us with food for our needs and herbs for healing. And have we not been able to benefit from these herbs? Have they not been a blessing to many people? In my practice many would go without proper treatment if it was not for the most marvellous source of healing powers which God has endowed to herbs and roots. In some cases even little leaves can help human suffering and enable us to sometimes overcome seemingly incurable diseases.

Earlier in this chapter I have mentioned the miracle of a baby's birth. How wonderful it is that simple herbs could perform a potential miracle on a man who wanted to father his own child!

In one of the Manchester papers I read about a young man whose eyesight had been severely affected. The article was accompanied by a beautiful photograph of his daughter and himself. The headlines read: "Herbs saved my sight when I refused an operation", and the article continued: "Six months ago I watched with special interest my baby daughter at play. I knew that I was losing my sight and therefore wanted to store as many visual memories of her as possible. Now, at the age of 22, I can look forward to seeing my daughter grow up following a remarkable course of herbal treatment to which I owe my sight."

It went on to say that this man had given up all hope of retaining his sight and that, twelve months previously, the doctors had told him that he would lose his sight unless he had a cornea transplant. Because of his religious beliefs, he did not want a transplant and his sight gradually deteriorated. He was forced to sell his business because he could no longer safely climb ladders and he started to learn braille. He also began to use a white walking-stick to help him across the road. At that point his mother-in-law suggested that he should visit me.

I told him that I had never treated a case like his before, but after counselling I prescribed him some herbal remedies. Five months later his eyesight was much improved. He stopped his braille lessons and now he can read for an hour without trouble, although some days his vision still blurs.

He is delighted with the improvement and considers the

best part of all is that he is able to watch his nine-month-old daughter. The eye tissue is getting better and the danger of going blind is diminishing. His ophthalmic surgeon is still sceptical about the progress, but the evidence is undeniable. He did state, however, that he was amazed and that in a career spanning 40 years he had never come across a case like this.

Once again nature had surprised everyone and come up trumps. What had seemed an impossibility became possible due to treatment which originated from nature. I am kept up to date about this young man's progress and I thank God for the natural healing powers which can activate or stimulate that great life force within us. For centuries it has displayed a surprising strength if it is applied correctly.

Sometimes when I am nonplussed by a case I turn to Mother Nature and ask for advice. If we are prepared to listen she never fails to tell us what to do and when I look at the results obtained, which are reminiscent of miracles, I appreciate all over again that nature *is* a healing miracle.

One of my older patients was left with a nasty wound after an operation, which frequently suppurated and would not heal. It had caused him a lot of pain and discomfort over a period of two-and-a-half years and nothing seemed to ease the situation. He was very distressed when he came to me and after having taken stock of his condition, I decided to put him on a course of Oil of Evening Primrose, consisting of capsules containing oil extracted from the seeds of the Evening Primrose.

Soon after starting the treatment two stitches, which had not been removed after his operation, loosened themselves and the wound was cleansed. The patient was relieved of all the pain and discomfort which he had suffered unnecessarily for two-and-a-half years. These simple seeds contain a life force so strong that it is capable of fighting off outside influences.

Do we need any further convincing of the importance of obeying the laws of nature, which are equivalent to the laws of God?

7

Witchcraft and Demonic Possession

IT SEEMS that in the last few years all kinds of healing crafts have been put under the one umbrella of "Alternative Medicine". I find it quite astonishing, when I attend certain alternative medicine conferences or seminars, that I hear about various doubtful healing practices. Travelling throughout the world I have seen that even witchcraft is placed under the umbrella of alternative medicine. I find this a sad reflection on the field of alternative medicine, as this combination is totally unwarranted and unacceptable.

With all my years of experience in this area I find it totally out of order that the phenomenon of witchcraft is classified in this particular category. Certain older publications on the subject of witchcraft try to create the idea that hunger, illness or death was caused by being bewitched. Nowadays, unfortunately, it is being suggested that witchcraft can be directed to a great healing purpose.

Most people still associate witchcraft with old women armed with black cats, who might, with the aid of a crystal ball, look into the future and perhaps bring about certain healing. Nobody would deny that certain ailments may disappear supposedly due to witchcraft, but let us never forget that witchcraft is directed by devilish powers, which do still exist today.

In the Middle Ages, we learn that certain rules came into existence, aimed at banning the devilish powers which reigned in many parts of the world. The old-fashioned witch, nevertheless, was especially well known during the time of the Reformation. From history we find that in the fifteenth, sixteenth and seventeenth centuries there was a great upsurge of witchcraft all over Europe, when, if so inclined, one would receive certain powers by vowing allegiance to the Devil. The number of victims who had anything to do with witchcraft in this period was horrendous and it is said that about one million people were executed throughout the world because they were supposed to be witches.

The theory exists that a witch will not be aware of what he or she is doing, especially when working on certain future ideas. Although it is a long time since the last black witch was judged in court, we find today that witchcraft is surging its way back in a weird and unnatural display of strength. Very often it is displayed to impress on people that white magic is designed for our benefit and magic powers are used to convince us of this.

It is a fallacy to believe that in previous generations people would not consider the subject rationally. The problem was that witchcraft was misunderstood and fear was instilled in its subjects in order to win over converts.

Voodoo, a popular religion in Haiti, was based on extreme fear and during the ceremonies and the celebrations to inaugurate the priests there were many tests of fire which lasted for days.

Today, even in the UK, we see witchcraft returning and it is a growing phenomenon that witches are taking possession of empty churches. The largest covens are said to be in the area of Prestwick in Scotland.

In African countries we can still see that witch doctors hold a position of power. Many African communities worship and revere these witch doctors as gods.

All over the world witches are congregating again and all with the same zeal as Christians exert to serve God. These witches are worshipping the Devil as their god and this is creating discord all over the world.

The sad part of this new development is that witchcraft is at present largely seen to be focused towards aiding human suffering with the healing powers which are at hand. Successes obtained by these powers might be regarded by the simpler souls as harmless, but they generally are not aware of that, or of whom they are worshipping. The dangers in this particular field should never be underestimated.

Recently I read in the diary of a witch that she was fully aware of her powers, with which she would be able to help society to recover from its spiritual inertia and disbelief. The diary ends: "If the crystal ball, the decks of tarot cards and ouija boards give some success to an increasingly vast population in search of something better in the future, who can deny their usefulness?"

It seems a noble idea when we read those words, but one cannot deny that, as the Bible teaches us, the Devil comes as "an angel of light", which is much more dangerous than when he comes to us as a "breezing lion".

Throughout history we read about witches who are referred to variously as wizards, warlocks, conjurers, necromancers, sorcerers, magicians or simply as "super witch". They all try with their different methods to sway people towards their powers—which seem to reign today more than ever before in our history.

Another group is at present rearing its head and these are the Satanists. They congregate in big groups and are vowed to secrecy. Whoever reveals any of their secret practices will be killed. Occasionally large gatherings of devil-worshippers will meet in utter secrecy and frequently money and blackmail is involved in these particular exercises.

Not so long ago we witnessed the trial of someone who used the money of innocent people for the purpose of the uncovering of Satanism and ridding the world of Satanists.

In the *Daily Mirror* of Wednesday 12 March 1986 we read, also, of how the police snatched a twelve-year-old girl from the arms of her mother, who was suspected of witchcraft. The police had been informed of black magic practices and had used a sledgehammer to break down the door of the woman's flat.

A reporter heard the mother's hysterical screaming in the background as her boyfriend explained what was happening. Then the police and two social workers burst in and whisked the girl away. Throughout the 3am police operation the mother behaved in a hysterical manner and when her daughter was grabbed she started chanting the Lord's Prayer.

It was all very spooky. The hall porter at the block of flats in Chelsea, London, said that the couple were deeply religious, yet Scotland Yard later confirmed the allegations that witchcraft and black magic lay behind the raid.

Every now and then we read of this sort of occurrence which is growing evidence that witchcraft is again sweeping the world.

It is sad, however, to see that because people seem to be intrigued by the word "miracle", these witches try to display some miraculous feats of which they are capable with their devilish powers, and so succeed in misleading innocent people.

While I was preparing this particular chapter, I was reminded of a young man who had consulted me a few years ago. His face had borne a seemingly permanently shocked expression and he could hardly sit still on his chair. He informed me that he had an unusual problem. After having listened to him I looked him straight in the eye and asked if he had told me everything. He shrugged his shoulders, was quiet for a moment and then blurted out: "Doctor, do you believe in evil powers?"

I answered that I most certainly did, but wondered what it had to do with his problem.

He responded: "If you are open-minded, maybe I am allowed to tell you the whole story. A few years ago I was working as a bartender in London and I became interested in tarot cards. These tarot cards have some secret signs for which special knowledge is required and I was intrigued and got more deeply involved than I intended. I got mixed up with a group of people I would not otherwise have associated with, and gradually I got sucked in deeper and deeper.

"Suddenly one evening, a gentleman, whom I had never met before, entered the bar. He was completely sober and out of the blue he asked me if I was interested in tarot card readings, which I confirmed hesitantly. Then he warned me and offered to tell me about his experiences, which might serve as a deterrent to never dabble again in the dangerous practices of involvement with tarot cards."

My patient then continued with the story he heard from his customer. The man claimed that one day he was approached by a lady and it was not until later he discovered she was a witch. Their conversation strayed on to the subject of witchcraft and tarot cards. Eventually it came to a disagreement.

By this time the man had realised that there was more to this particular lady than had at first met the eye. After their disagreement they parted, but not before the witch had cursed him and doomed him to death. He went home and that same night he suffered severe internal bleedings. He was taken to hospital in a desperate condition and had to undergo several operations before he was declared out of danger. My patient had seen the scars and told me they reminded him of a patch-work quilt. He was left in no doubt that he had been told the truth.

Much to the surprise of the surgeons and doctors the man in question managed to live through this particular incident, but none of them believed his story. Not long after his recovery he heard that the witch had died, because her spell had been broken. As he had lived through her curse she was destined to die.

After relating this story the strange visitor left the bar with another warning that my patient should no longer dabble in tarot-card readings or something was bound to happen to him as well. Whatever the reason may be, the next day my patient started to suffer from a skin disease which to this day has been incurable.

Because this gentleman had been honest with me and had told me the whole story, I thought that I might possibly be able to take that curse away from him. I felt that perhaps with some natural medicine we might be able to turn the tide.

This particular incident happened a few years ago and my patient has not been able to sit in comfort since, which just goes to show how frighteningly powerful witchcraft can be.

Some people continue to believe those kind of events only occur in the Far East, and would be surprised to realise that they happen all around us. I have been approached for treatment quite a few times by people who had been in the hands of so-called witches and they require a lot of counselling as well as spiritual guidance.

These powers originated from Creation and having been wrested away and adopted by the Devil, have grown stronger. Paul gives us a clear warning in his letter to the Ephesians (6: 12):

> For we are not fighting against human beings but against the wicked spiritual forces in the heavenly world, the rulers, authorities, and cosmic powers of this dark age.

This concludes that the world rulers of darkness and the spiritual host of wickedness are very powerful in heavenly places. They wrestle against flesh and blood and let us never lose sight of the spiritual side of human beings. The only way we can help ourselves is to arm ourselves with the equipment advised to us in that same sixth chapter of Ephesians.

I was once told the true story of some people who were in business in the Far East. Because of envy, a voodoo spell was placed on the owner and his wife by their competitors. The husband fell seriously ill because of this voodoo, but his wife was never affected. It was discovered that because the woman was a true believer and worshipper of God, she was unaffected by the devilish powers of the voodoo spell placed on her. Again we see the strength of God's powers in a fight between good and evil.

In many African countries the people's faith is placed in the witch doctor, whose position is maintained by fear and based on magic. Millions of people choose to attend a witch doctor instead of going for good, sound medical help. When I was lecturing throughout that part of the world, I had an interesting experience myself, which proved to me that these powers are very often useless.

I had the privilege of sitting in on a seminar on a newly developed method which often gives the impression of magic. This is the magneto therapy, where we can balance energies in the body by using copper and zinc magnets. The British Bio-Magnetic Association has scientifically studied the process of how copper and zinc magnets can be applied to balance energy, using certain acupuncture points. The results of this kind of treatment are sometimes considered as miracles by those who have benefited from the treatment.

One of the people I got to know in Africa was almost crippled by rheumatics and, as an osteopathic practitioner, I was immediately aware that most of his problems were caused by an irregularity in his pelvic region. One of his legs was considerably shorter than the other. I asked him to do me a favour and take me to the witch doctor who had treated him. He did not hold with other doctors and actually visited his witch doctor quite frequently.

Medically trained people justifiably dislike witch doctors because of the damage caused to their so-called patients. It needed rather a lot of persuasion before my coloured friend consented to take me along. When we arrived there, the witch doctor was far from happy to see me. I told him that I was very interested in his working methods and asked him if he could balance my friend's pelvic area, as the difference in the length of his legs was quite clearly visible.

The witch doctor took a red-hot poker out of the fire and used this on every centimetre of my friend's shorter leg.

There are many people who think that these witch doctors do a marvellous job because their patients are released from pain. It is true to say that if enough pain is caused and perhaps certain acupuncture points are touched, endorphins and encephalins are released and these people might temporarily be freed from pain. The fact that they are scarred for life seems to be of very little importance!

After this horrifying "treatment", I asked the witch doctor to measure my friend's legs. My friend obliged by moving them up and down to see if they were balanced and by stretching them. There was not one centimetre of improvement. When I asked him if he knew any other methods, he threw a handful of bones into the air and told us that the patient should now be all right. He became impatient when I asked him to re-measure the legs, because again there was no change.

As a white man I was not allowed to touch the patient, but I asked the witch doctor to place the zinc and copper magnets I handed him on certain points of the pelvic area. I would give him the exact locations without touching the patient. He was anxious to learn how this method would work and agreed. I showed him the points and the magnets were put in position while I prayed to the one and only God.

When my friend put his weight on his legs, stretched them and walked around, the imbalance in the pelvic area was corrected and the legs were near enough the same length.

The witch doctor was utterly amazed and deeply impressed. He asked me what he had to do to learn this art. I told him that first he would have to learn about acupuncture. He would have to acquire the scientific knowledge related to this treatment and then he would be able to work with these magnets. Alternatively he could follow a course in the bio-magnetic fields.

Although both the witch doctor and my friend were impressed by the results, and my friend in particular was more than happy, I told him that if he paid more attention to his diet, he would benefit further. I was pleased when some time later I received a Christmas card from him with the extra information that he was feeling well and had not experienced any further problems.

The witch doctor's powers had failed and we again must realise that energy is found in nature which, if properly applied, is not just harmless, but greatly beneficial.

After many years working as an alternative practitioner it makes me very sad to realise that today we have reached the stage where healing sometimes is done in the name of witchcraft.

There are various forms of healing with which we should be careful. For centuries magicians or students of the occult have used instruments such as pendulums, crystal balls or magic mirrors to contact higher powers in order to gain possession of divine powers.

The pendulum, derived from the divining rod, the crystal ball and the magic mirror, stimulates hypnotic conditions and some paranormal abilities may come to the surface. But these seemingly innocent practices have also caused some very dangerous conditions.

I remember when a young girl was brought into our clinic early one morning. She was still totally under the hypnotic influence of a stage hypnotist who had used a pendulum and a crystal ball in the name of entertainment. He had brought her so deeply under his influence, that he had found it impossible to get her out of her trance.

They had tried everything to awaken her, even slapping her face and eventually she had partly recovered. It was in that dazed condition she was brought to me the next morning. She looked years older than her age and was in a pitiful state.

Luckily, some of the methods I used on her worked and she came out of her trance. Together with some guidance, I gave her a few of the Bach flower remedies and Dr Vogel's herbal remedies and succeeded by these natural means to bring about her total awakening.

I remember, however, a similar case in the Netherlands,

where the girl never regained consciousness. For a long time she was fed intravenously, hoping that she would eventually return to consciousness. Unfortunately this never happened. The powers which are given to us are gifts from God and cannot be handled with carelessness and opportunism.

Today we also see the rise of demonic possession. This is a growing problem and it is a fallacy that a human personality cannot be possessed by demons. In my practice alone I have come across quite a few cases over the years.

It is often stated that there are no such things as demons, but even back in Biblical days we read about spirits which are opposed to God and can cause immense harm. Especially during my research for this book I have found that many of these demonic powers have been rediscovered. They are, however, not often talked about.

Do not underestimate the danger of demonic possession, because many people have been driven into mental institutions as a result of them. They have also caused irreparable damage to people's physical health. We should always be on our guard and, although we might be ignorant of any danger, more damage is done by demonic possession than one could ever have believed possible.

I remember that quite some time ago a well-known clairvoyant came to me for treatment. I took her to one of the treatment rooms where she had previously undergone treatment. This time, however, when she entered the room she started to shiver all over and shouted and cried for help. I could make out that she was sensing a demonic power which was threatening her.

Under any other circumstances I would have been very surprised, but I immediately realised that shortly before a demonised person had been in that room who had consulted me, even though he had not been sincerely interested in help.

Never in my life have I witnessed a battle of demonic powers so fierce and tremendous as that particular day. I doubt that I will ever forget the experience and I certainly hope never to have to witness anything like it again. It took me a long time before I managed to bring this clairvoyant to her senses again.

I am always surprised when I hear of naïve people who delve into these powers without any knowledge of the background or of the risks involved.

Even any belongings or possessions of a demonic person should be removed as far away as possible, as the energy in these belongings might affect the individual for the worse. They might contain an energy which could have a detrimental influence.

Not just great demonic individuals such as Satan, Lucifer or Beelzebub deserve a cautious mention, but also demonised people who might pass through our lives. If the devil enters and pervades people with the influences of the supernatural and the unknown, certain obsessions could result which will affect the sound thinking and actions of those under that influence.

In history we come across many famous cases of demonic possession. We should know that it is not just confined to the past, but unfortunately is still happening. In different ways the demons are still active and they have been the cause of untold misery, hysteria and mental illness to those who do not worship the true God.

My old friend, Dr Sanchez-Perez, in one of his books, *Engrammes of the Universe*, writes about the still little-known system of nervous fibres, located in the tenuous outermost layer of the arteries, called the adventitia. He mentions the corpuscles of Pacini and the arteriovenous glomic anastomosis, whose purpose has not yet been discovered.

These may be the receiving or transmitting organs for these forces that are still not understood, although there is no doubt about their existence. By correlating all this information and research, we may come to understand the phenomena which have been observed and described in a number of ways. Although we have been given multiple and diverse explanations, these could basically be different aspects of one and the same phenomenon. Very little is known as yet about these areas. There also exists areas which are controlled by God and we must be selective in our allegiance.

We often see difficulties arising if the control of parapsychology is lacking in its objective theories. I am often asked why I am so wary and cautious of certain methods. My reply usually is that we should work with the gifts that God has put within our reach, but when it comes to those which are beyond our reach, we take a tremendous responsibility in our hands if we enter into the undiscovered.

Maybe this is the reason, when I am asked if I believe in the Christian biblical principles, I say that the Bible, to my mind, is the only document which has given us the right revelations. Christ was the image of what He preached with regard to this and He lived to the letter of the laws laid down in the Old Testament, which He was able to fulfil in the New Testament through His lifestyle here on earth.

Our Christian beliefs, both in the East and in the West, are not lacking in documentation, that is to say Biblical knowledge. This indeed has been reaffirmed by recent discoveries of the Dead Sea scrolls, which give us yet more proof. Out of these beliefs miracles have been worked, which in themselves are a support and guide in times of need, when demonic powers seem to be overwhelming us.

I remember some time ago that a lady from a nearby town came to me, totally confused and completely out of touch with reality. For some time she had been unable to relate rationally to her family and was referred by her doctor to a psychiatrist, who had advised her family that she should be treated in a psychiatric hospital.

She had undergone an experience in her life for which she certainly had not volunteered, but unfortunately it had left her possessed or demonised. She had degenerated and eventually grown out of touch with her everyday existence. The poor soul looked like a frightened little bird and her anxiety never let up. Thank goodness it is not often that I see such a pathetic creature, for in no way could I get any sense out of her. I tried to help her, but nothing seemed to work.

When she arrived for her third visit, I was very busy and my friend, Dr Hans Moolenburgh from the Netherlands, was staying with me. He is a general practitioner, but I know that he has also helped demonically possessed people. I was sure that he would proceed very carefully, so I asked him to see her.

He asked me for a quiet room, where he took the lady and spent approximately one hour with her. When she came out, her face had assumed a completely different expression. From her previously imprisoned face she now looked much more freely into the world and seemed relieved from a great burden. After she had left, I asked my friend how on earth he had managed to bring about such a change.

He told me that in his experience the finest method to free people possessed by the Devil, was to read Psalm 91 over and over again. Having read out this particular Bible passage repeatedly, he then let the possessed person read it through. Initially it will go haltingly until he or she fully understands the uplifting words and often as a result the person will be freed from the demonic possession. The power of God's words will drive out the demonic power of Satan.

I never actually saw this lady again, but often wondered what had become of her. It was five years later that the same lady phoned me and asked if it was at all possible to put her in touch with Dr Moolenburgh, as he was the only person who had managed to free her from that "strange spirit", as she called it.

I asked her what had happened and she told me that after her session with Dr Moolenburgh she had entered a new lease of life and been completely free. Recently, however, she had again been in contact with what she called some devilish powers and the whole thing had started all over again.

I told her about the method Dr Moolenburgh had followed and she said that she had forgotten which Psalm they had read to each other. After giving her the required information, she phoned me back later to inform me that the miracle had been performed again and she was once more released from her possession.

It would have been so easy to institutionalise a person like her, but that would not have cured her. Possibly psychiatric treatment might have had the required result, but that remains to be seen.

In holistic medicine the whole, individual patient should be regarded and we should remember what the great philosopher Plato said:

> The great error in the treatment of the human body is that physicians separate the soul or spirit from the body.

Medicines often fail, while guidance and counselling in these matters frequently may provide the key to seemingly miraculous events.

8

Devil-dancing

ON A BEAUTIFUL summer's evening some years ago, after working most of the day in a general hospital in Colombo, Sri Lanka, I was invited together with some friends to witness one of the greatest manifestations I have seen in my life.

The centuries-old ritual of devil-dancing is still being practised in Sri Lanka. Its purpose is to chase away the devils when illness occurs and it is the ancient belief in Sri Lanka that illness constitutes an affliction of the devil. In several of their temples they still practise ceremonies to chase the devils away and the particular ceremony we were allowed to witness was most impressive.

Hundreds of people were gathered outside the temple, which was a beautiful old building situated between the lovely trees and flowers of the island. The priest had separated the crowd into different parties to help the two seriously ill people who were to be the subjects of the ceremony. Only that morning I had spoken with one of the two people to be treated there and I was aware of the fact that he did not have long to live.

When everybody was seated or had found a place, the ceremony started. Several of the young men who took part used tambourines along with some other instruments and danced and sang. With the almost unbelievable noises they produced, they intended to chase the devils away.

The priests witnessed the dancing and at the altar they chanted their prayers and brought sacrifices. In this almost indescribable atmosphere the first patient was brought forward and seated. This was the man with whom I had spoken that morning and he was around the age of 70. He suffered from a malignant stomach cancer, which was inoperable because of the severity of his condition and he had pinned his hopes on this ritual.

Amid loud prayers and singing and dancing he was prepared for the practitioner. Our friend, Professor Anton Jayasuriya, who is a surgeon at the general hospital in Colombo, had previously shown us the X-rays of both patients who would be the centre of the ritual that night. These X-rays were studied by several of the doctors present and they clearly showed the malignant tumour, which was so large that the man could neither eat nor drink. Any food or drink came back up again within seconds.

The practitioner started by putting his hands on the man's stomach, then on his chest and meanwhile danced around him. Then two of the devil dancers brought him a silver plate on which lay sections of limes. The practitioner took some of these fruit segments and rubbed these on to the chest of the patient, while in the background the wild dancing continued. This ritual lasted for quite some time.

Where the patient had originally looked ashen, we saw that some colour was slowly returning to his cheeks. He was then invited to eat a banana and some coconut and this he munched with visible enjoyment. He swallowed the food and looked a different man when he later left the platform.

I had the opportunity of seeing him again before I left Sri Lanka and he was indeed in a greatly improved condition.

The second man was around the age of 50. Again, through our friend Professor Jayasuriya, we saw his X-rays. He also suffered from a tumour; although it was not malignant, it was so large that he was unable to eat and therefore his days were numbered. He had already lost a great deal of weight and looked emaciated.

The same performance took place and this time I also watched the faces of the bystanders, which clearly expressed their approval and appreciation of the whole ritual. The singing and dancing continued in the background and the swollen tumour in the man's throat was clearly visible. More limes were brought to rub over the patient's chest and throat and as this took place we could actually see the tumour shrink. He had not been able to eat for many weeks and when offered a banana, which is not too easily digested, he ate it with relish.

Before he left the temple this man came along to see us, so that we could all verify that the tumour had disappeared. My wife and I had witnessed this whole procedure and we had to admit that a miracle had taken place. But this is not the end of the story.

After the ceremony we left that beautiful part of Sri Lanka and later in the evening we attended a typical Sri Lankan house party. We were sitting talking about this incredible experience when we were joined by a gentleman. My wife looked at him and suddenly said: "You look like the practitioner who was in charge of the ceremony tonight." She then continued doubtfully: "But did I not see you at work in the hospital as well this morning?"

He admitted that he was the practitioner involved at the ritualistic ceremony and also that he was a consultant at the general hospital. In utter amazement we asked him why he should ever recommend the use of a scalpel if people could be cured by way of the ceremony which we had witnessed that night.

He chuckled and replied that in the first place it was a very difficult ceremony to perform. I must admit that it had been clearly noticeable how much the ritual had taken out of him. These ceremonial exercises are very taxing and we had seen the sweat pouring off him during the ceremony.

He told us that not everybody was willing to partake in these ceremonies, which had been handed down by many generations over centuries. Certain cases seemed to benefit from this ritual but the patients had to be spiritually prepared for it and therefore it was often easier to use the more modern methods available.

We were obviously very interested in his revelations and spent an interesting evening with him. He assured us that both patients would be all right as the ritual rarely fails to work.

Some time later during that evening a group of young men joined the party. They started to perform certain rituals which were also designed to chase away devils. There were also fire-eaters and snake-charmers. When I saw the enormous burning torches of these fire-eaters, which they moved over their bodies and also put into their mouths, I could not resist the opportunity to talk to some of them. When I expressed my doubt and wondered if it was cold fire, I was invited to test for myself—and burned my fingers in the process!

So from painful experience I learned that this was real fire and that they seemed to be able to control the fire and use it whichever way they wanted. The fire did not harm their bodies, which remained totally unmarked.

I asked them how they managed to do this and they, too, chuckled to each other. The members of this particular group were all related to each other and they told me that the secret had been handed down for so many generations that even they did not know exactly how and why it worked. They continued with their dancing and fire-eating performances which left us spellbound.

Our friend, who had performed the miraculous healings in the temple smiled at me when I returned to our group after my experiment with the burning torch and confirmed that many rituals had been handed down from ancient times and these were completely inexplicable. The fact that these rituals were still being performed today and that this knowledge is not lost in our modern times, is certainly beneficial, but the big question must be where the powers used originate from.

When I asked him to whom he accredited the power, his answer was that the great master Buddha had apportioned such powers, which were beyond explanation.

The next day we had the chance to witness another ritual which took place at a meeting attended by hundreds of people. Again this was designed to cure ailing people. The patient concerned in this ceremony suffered from severe back problems and we watched while four sharp hooks were fastened into his flesh, without any form of anaesthetic, but the patient never showed any signs of pain.

Ropes were fastened on to these hooks and from the four corners of his body he was elevated by a pulley so that the hundreds of spectators could witness him hanging there. Still no visible signs of pain were noticeable. While he was suspended there he managed to wave his hand at us, as if to reassure us that he was not uncomfortable.

When he was brought down he was laid on a bench and along with some of the other medical people who had witnessed the ceremony, we were invited to look for marks left by the sharp hooks which had been put into his body. To our complete amazement we could not detect any marks, in fact no signs of blood whatsoever. The victim assured us that he had not felt any pain and that his back was now fine.

There is a little village outside Colombo, Sri Lanka, where about 40 practitioners live. These could be classified as alternative practitioners, by whom people from all over the world have been treated with the use of different ancient practices. These methods used to alleviate sickness have been handed down over many generations.

One practitioner was blind and he would know what to do and what not to do with a patient by intuition or instinct. The treatments he performed were indeed almost like miracles.

This beautifully situated little village is an excellent example of knowledge having been preserved from ancient civilisations. Healing practices have been performed here over many centuries and even today some of these practices seem again able to capture our imagination.

The Sri Lankan government has recently appointed a Minister for Indigenous Medicine in an effort to save many of these ancient rituals and ceremonies; to research and further develop them. The focus is on the individual choice of the patient being entitled to choose which form of treatment he or she would prefer to undergo. It is each and everyone's individual responsibility to decide for themselves the origin of the power which makes these treatments possible.

I am personally all in favour of researching ancient methods, especially the wealth of knowledge of herbal medicine in these old civilisations. Many people have benefited from this knowledge and much may be gained from keeping it alive.

Nature is a wonderful source of health and it more than fulfils the Creator's promise that herbs would be available for healing.

I have had the opportunity of studying and learning from several ancient civilisations on my travels all over the world. Sometimes I have been surprised by their mystique, but also by their common sense. In the days before medical knowledge as we know it, our forebears used intuitive healing practices. With our modern communications we ought to consider ourselves lucky that we can now draw on their experiences.

Recently I met a very old practitioner who is based in Pakistan. He told me that only a short while ago three ancient tribes in Pakistan were discovered, whose healing methods, developed over many generations, had been previously unknown. These methods are largely based on plants and roots and their traditional rituals are based on many natural ingredients. It seems that even modern problems such as AIDS may be successfully treated by some of their extracts from roots and plants.

Once again we are made to realise that in our modern times many things still remain a mystery and that somewhere there is still a wealth of untapped knowledge. Contrary to general opinion, science has not really overtaken the wonder of nature and it would be wise to set aside some grants or financial aid for research into these unknown ancient methods, proven over centuries and now superseded by our modern technology.

9

Modern Miracles

VERY OFTEN during presentations, whether it be to students or to the general public, the question is put to me of how I see the future of medicine. Mostly my answer is that, although we are passing through a difficult time, it nevertheless is a very interesting period. Old practices, treatments and remedies, which may have lain dormant for a long time, are being rediscovered and brought to light and we are obliged to investigate them. Today we can call them "modern miracles" because they have been forgotten.

One other point I always stress is that we have only scratched the surface of knowledge regarding the many natural forces, which we bundle together under the term "energy".

Energy embraces everything, and everything is based on energy. All matter, thought and emotion is energy. We live in a world of energy and we are an integral part of these energies. It is high time that, as individuals, we accept the responsibility of our bodies, thought and emotions, which all relate to our health.

Our energy is the sum total of all that we think, feel, eat or achieve during our lifetime. Energy, however, changes from one minute to the next and it is important to flow *with* these energies, to be aware and to utilise them for the benefit of our mind, body and spirit.

I remember when only a few months ago I walked with Professor Arthur J. Ellison in the Cathedral of Cologne. Out of the blue I suddenly asked him: "Arthur, have you ever seen a miracle or have you ever experienced a miracle? And what do you consider is a miracle?"

I will never forget his answer. After a moment's consideration he replied: "Life is a miracle and whenever we can discover our own energies and get in tune with these energies, we have performed a miracle."

This I have so often found to be true. Through energy, which may itself be called a "miracle", we have been able to discover many ways in which an apparent impossibility can be achieved.

In medicine, for instance, energy has often been applied with amazing results. If we go back a long time and look at the Indian, Chinese, Greek or Arabian civilisations and consider the individual ways of thinking of their great philosophers, we realise that medicine is closely related to religion and philosophy. During the Renaissance period, however, medicine became a separate science, detaching itself from religion and later from philosophy as well. Medicine then became more scientific.

The practice of medicine became increasingly more materialistic and scientific and in that process some of the essential life forces for our health were being overlooked. Energy is part and parcel of the life essentials.

Scientists today are incorrect in their belief that the basic laws of nature have been discovered and that we have a full understanding of these laws, because the basic law of energy still remains a mystery.

Some Soviet scientists recently found that the human brain centres and transmits on a combined wavelength in centimetres, millimetres and micron ranges. This proves that a lot more investigation needs to be, and is being, done today.

It is high time that we could see a new understanding of physiology being accepted, which would include all life forms and accept cosmic energy as a prime force for life and its functions. Disease can then be brought back to what it once was: a deviation or imbalance from the norm. Over the last few centuries great discoveries have been made in physics, medicine and chemistry and we are hopefully moving towards this better understanding.

In his excellent book, *The Pattern of Health*, Dr Aubrey T. Westlake said that all miracles cannot be claimed to be fact. If we aim to find a definition of a "miracle", it is a necessity that authentic records be kept.

Firstly, with an acute disease the process of restoring normality needs to be speeded up until the time element is completely eliminated for this to qualify as a "modern miracle". Secondly, with chronic or incurable diseases it is the immediate restarting of the process of regeneration and restoration to normality which counts. Finally, it is clear that lacking careful diagnostic data, we cannot claim that all "miracles" are in fact miracles.

Modern medicine has given us the opportunity of using new techniques for medical diagnosis. Amongst other techniques, the radioactive isotope gives us the capability of exploration of almost every part of the human body. Present-day technology has also supplied us with techniques which enable us to perform intricate surgery.

Great advances have been made, not only in orthodox medicine, but also in the alternative or complementary medicine and some of this newly acquired knowledge is a refined version of old and established methods. Some of the techniques now available to us could be applied to create potential "miracles".

Among the newer methods let us look at the Energy Emission Analysis. This method can be used for body energy analysis and therapeutic intervention and control. It can give us statistical records of changes in the energy emissions which regularly occur with respect to the disease process and can thereby lead to a therapeutic intervention.

The interpretation of Energy Emission Analysis in the entire energy emission gives information on all the energy fields and the negative signs as well as their relationships with each other.

With some of the modern techniques we receive information on colour, on light and on energy, and with these energetic phenomena we can exhibit alterations long before a disease clinically manifests itself.

I recently saw a new machine demonstrated. It was developed by Professor Vincent and the machine can detect early signs of cancer. Moreover, during treatment of a cancer patient, the progress of treatment for better or worse, can be followed quite closely on this particular machine. I call it a modern miracle that through our observations it becomes evident, long before symptoms manifest themselves, that bodily changes, disease or illness are energetically existent and reveal themselves through our photographic techniques.

The bio-energy within individuals represents information on normal harmonious energy flow and cell functions. Among the techniques available to us today we have the Vega machine, the Mora machine and the Dermatron machine, and these represent great hope for the future in enabling us to help patients efficiently.

One of my patients had suffered with her health for many years. Her problem seemingly was an after-effect from a disease she had previously suffered. Although she had been assured by the medical profession that the treatment had been successful and the disease was now completely under control, she had never been the same again. It had undermined her health and I decided to use the Dermatron machine which was developed by Dr Voll.

On the basis of the informative energy at the beginning and end points of the classical acupuncture meridians, it took less than five minutes with this machine before I found the problem. Within two weeks this particular lady had improved so much that she referred to her treatment as a "miracle".

After feeling below par for such a long time, she once more enjoyed good health.

The Western practitioner is trained to analytically look only into the theory of cause and effect. They have not been taught the theory which was founded several millenia ago in the time of the Yellow Imperium:

Where is the energy blocked?
Which is the weak area?
Where is excess energy?
Where can the energy be balanced?

Working with a modern form of acupuncture, i.e. the electro-acupuncture, we realise that this technique truly deserves the substitute name of a "modern miracle". So many people have been treated successfully by electro-acupuncture where orthodox treatment had failed.

With great respect to the Chinese who have worked with acupuncture for approximately 5,000 years, the modern electro-acupuncture is a synthesis of Western medicine, electronic power and classical acupuncture. The stimulation produced by electro-acupuncture can cause the energy in the human body to be balanced.

Dr Voll, the founder of electro-acupuncture, introduced, after detailed research, his own methods to stimulate the acupuncture points that balance energy. He started with the knowledge of the Chinese, who used these particular points as long as 3,000 years ago. Through this technique we can come to clinical diagnosis in a quicker and more efficient way.

Another modern miracle is kinesiology or muscle-testing. Here we have a tool for identifying precisely what is taking place in a patient's nervous system, relying on a method of sophisticated body bio-feedback communication. Kinesiology has only been utilised for standard muscle testing at the patient's pectoral major clavicular division since the sixties. These procedures have now been refined to the point where muscle-testing provides a consistently accurate control in assessing patients' health problems—a line of communication with the patient's nervous system.

Muscles and organs have specific viscero-somatic and somaticovisceral relationships. This technique enables the location of a malfunction to be found very quickly. Kinesiology has worked for some patients like a miracle because it may detect allergies which have sometimes affected a patient's health for many years. It is a very simple diagnostic tool which unveils the body/brain factor and places this in perspective and therefore another new development or perhaps modern miracle of this age which may be utilised with great benefit.

The developments in the enzyme therapy, a modern medicine without side-effects, has also produced some miraculous results. It has proven especially invaluable in the field of incurable degenerative diseases.

And we must not forget nature, our very best friend, who has delivered natural medicines which have been available for centuries and centuries and about which we still learn new applications today.

My friend, Dr Alfred Vogel, the great researcher of herbal applications, has over the past fifty years added some wonderful, previously unknown herbal remedies to the list. In some cases these have been of help where other medicines had failed, because of the life force concentrated within them. Through the use of herbs, so effective a healing response has been brought forward, that it remains inexplicable. Life is indeed a miracle and I fully endorse what Professor Ellison said to me not so long ago.

One factor which has remained constant throughout the many changes in medicine, is the "placebo". The meaning of this old Latin word is "I shall please". A placebo effect is a healing with a neutral substance.

The process of the placebo effect is also one of the factors which, through its innate self-healing system, brings a response beyond explanation. Every interaction between patient and doctor has an element of that placebo effect, yet that process is still very much misunderstood. Despite the fact that placebo effects are pervasive, the avenues to understanding them are still largely unexplored.

Dr Joel Elkes from the University of Louisville (USA) describes this feature as follows: "I have never understood why so powerful an instrument of healing as the placebo could have been dismissed in arrogant disdain by our profession rather than being viewed as a precious resource deserving the most careful and thorough scrutiny."

How misunderstood this effect is by people who do not know anything about life forces or about the saying that everything affects everything else!

The modern scientist cannot understand and very often will not understand the great resources of this innate energy which lives in every living creature. If we can work with these energies, we will learn to understand the bodily workings so much better. We will also learn why homoeopathy, which affects that life force directly, can perform what so often looks like a miracle.

Nowadays, too, we are able to realise the enormous knowledge to be gathered on outflowing body energy, which can be shown photographically. This information can be seen in black and white by using Kirlian photography, a technique which may be considered another modern miracle.

Kirlian photography makes the complex subject of energy so much more explainable. In 1939 the Russian engineer Semijon Kirlian was repairing an electrotherapy machine in a research laboratory in the Ukraine. Purely by accident, he allowed his hand to move too close to a live electrode. The shock he received was accompanied by a brilliant flash of light given off by a large spark of electricity. This aroused his curiosity and Kirlian wondered what would happen if he placed a sheet of light-sensitive material in the path of the spark. Placing his own hand behind the piece of light-sensitive paper, he repeated his action and when he developed the film, Kirlian found strange streamer-like emanations surrounding the image of his fingertips.

On closer inspection, Kirlian found that each emanation

was seen to have a different radiation pattern. He was fascinated and set up tests in order to capture the energy aura of any living thing. Today, this particular therapy is being used successfully to find out where the energy flow is disturbed. It also assists in finding where acupuncture points or "energy points" can be used to either block or stimulate energy or a disharmony in the energy flow, as is required.

There are still many theoretical or practical difficulties in this area, but through modern developments more and more knowledge concerning the energy body aura or bioplasmic body becomes available. A flow of energy surrounds almost all living beings or things. What that energy is all about, we cannot yet fully explain.

A lot of claims made on Kirlian photography are not justified, as Professor Arthur J. Ellison has correctly stated. One thing we do know, however, is that it is a modern method in the study of energy—which is a new scientific field.

A very interesting case comes to mind where, thanks to Kirlian photography, we managed to help a patient whom we suspected to be suffering from schizophrenia. Kirlian photographs were made of his hands and feet and when the photographs were developed we discovered a double aura. One of the auras was very disturbed and we found irregular acupuncture points. We tried to analyse these and after further detailed discussions, which included the patient, we found that he was possessed by an alien power. Those demonic powers became evident in the irregular and confusing energy aura. We did everything we could to rectify the situation and after treatment the demonised power was eventually removed and a complete new energy flow became evident.

There still remains a tremendous amount of research to be done into this modern method, but there is little doubt in my mind that it will become one of the greatest discoveries which enable us to perform "modern miracles". I am sure that with its help many conflicting theories will become more evident, and so be reassessed, and that much knowledge may be gained regarding the subject of energy.

Einstein's theory of relativity eventually became the orthodoxy of a scientific world, where originally it had caused many conflicting theories. Just as the relativity theory initially had been rejected as inconceivable, this Kirlian method will no doubt win approval and consent once it has been allowed to prove its worth.

Once more I repeat that we live in an age when some mysterious phenomena become apparent that warrant thorough investigation. It is also an age in which we have to tread carefully, as many of these new findings are often tarred with the same brush.

What really are modern miracles? Let us just look around us at discoveries of new scientific techniques where so many things interrelate. Consider the microchip, which has enabled us to do away with vast machinery. This tiny little object has proven invaluable in research programmes in many different fields, and most of us have benefited in some way or another.

We live in a stimulating and exciting time with many new scientific developments, which enable us to perform treatments which possibly deserve the description of "modern miracles".

Let us, however, not forget that nature, in all its splendour is undoubtedly the most outstanding and permanent miracle given to us by God, one of which man still has little or no comprehension.

10

"Miracles" with Patients

A MIRACLE is always in the mind of the beholder and no form of medicine or belief will ever change this. Many a time I hear a patient's claim that through their treatment a miracle has been performed.

I always regard the word "miracle" with a big question mark. Sometimes, if we enquire what one had been suffering in order to be so miraculously cured from pain or discomfort, the answer is quite often indefinite. It is usually too easily claimed that "it was like a miracle". It may have seemed that events took an unexpected turn, but as I have said at the beginning of the book, it is mostly a question of cause and effect.

We learn at school that every action brings a reaction and if that reaction is for the better, an exceptional outcome might appear as a miracle. To the question of what really constitutes a miracle, each individual must answer for himself.

However, looking back over the years, having treated thousands of people, things have happened in my practice which may have created the impression of a miracle. I have had to look through some of the many testimonials I have received to refresh my memory. It is not my intention to fill this last chapter with reels of testimonials, but I do want to relate some case histories to give the reader some insight into the workings of an alternative therapies clinic. We must realise that people who come to our practice are often people who have been through the accepted medical channels of doctors, specialists and possibly hospitals before coming to us as a last resort.

It does not take an expert to recognise the maxim of some of our patients: "If we do not benefit, at least we will not come to any harm."

After failing to find the results the patient had looked for in orthodox medicine, sometimes he or she will improve rapidly with one of our methods and I do not deny that it is heart-warming to hear of their gratitude. To see a patient improve and recover ought to be the greatest aim and reward for any practitioner, rather than the financial remuneration. To know that the given treatment has been effective and to witness and share their delight when they pick up the threads again after sometimes lengthy suffering, is totally satisfying.

When working in the General Hospital in Colombo, Sri Lanka, I saw a patient who was slightly malformed and therefore experienced great difficulty in walking. I was instructed by the surgeon who was in charge of my training to use just one acupuncture needle. This was to be placed without further stimulation in a specific acupuncture point. The response of this particular lady was so dramatic that after treatment she got up and walked out as if she had never had walking problems in her life. She was totally exhilarated. I was also very impressed to see what could be achieved with just one single needle.

I have frequently come across quite amazing results after acupuncture treatment, not just in my own clinic, but elsewhere too. Especially in China I have witnessed what deserve to be referred to as "miracles"—dramatic cures which have been achieved with the ancient art of acupuncture.

I particularly remember one specific case in China. Having finished my studies and before leaving the country, I was invited to assist a very busy practitioner. One day a lady with Bell's Palsy (facial paralysis) and severe malformation of the face sought treatment. She had suddenly decided to seek a possible cure after she had lived with these problems for 17 years. In this case too, my mentor used only one needle, which he placed right behind the eye. I was really quite shocked when I saw where he placed the needle. He worked and pulsated that needle and when the treatment was finished and the needle removed, his patient could not believe the improvement she had undergone. The Bell's Palsy with which she had lived for so many years, had completely disappeared.

To Western acupuncturists, the ability to perform with only one needle and achieve such results is indeed almost like a miracle, because even according to the theory of acupuncture this is almost impossible.

Some of my patients have made claims to the media about supposed miracles after acupuncture treatment. These claims I do not endorse, but I am inclined to be overawed by some of the "miraculous" outcomes I have seen in the Third World where instant cures were witnessed after the appropriate placing of just one needle. However, we should always remain rational where claims of miracles are concerned. As said before, it is impossible to judge unless the whole background to the case is known.

I think in particular of an extremely capable footballer whose career was ended because of a bad injury. He has often claimed in public and to the media that it was like a miracle how, after two acupuncture treatment sessions, he regained the movement of his foot. His doctors were sceptical and claimed that the improvement would only be temporary, yet this man is still playing professional football and performs as well as ever on the football pitch.

I would also like to tell you about a girl I had been treating for Multiple Sclerosis. She had been diagnosed by her doctor and unfortunately was now unable to manage without a wheelchair. During her first treatment session of electroacupunture she reported sensations in her legs. She then asked me if I thought that she might even walk again and I told her to always have a positive mind on any treatment. She then said that the feelings in her legs were getting stronger and at the end of the treatment she asked for permission to try to stand up. She came off the treatment couch and indeed managed to stand.

At her second treatment I decided to place the needles in a totally different position than is normally recommended for her condition. After this treatment she was able to leave the premises without using a wheelchair. Was this a miracle? I have to leave the answer to that question to the reader, but she is still walking about. The result indeed was startling. The girl is still on her feet and able to walk and blesses the day she ever decided to come for that particular treatment.

Her doctor had discouraged her, as did her religious friends. When I spoke to her along the lines of the contents of this book, i.e. about faith and trust in Him who reigns over us all, she accepted the fact that it was not me who had helped her—she felt that God had used me as an instrument and had guided me to place the needles in the right place. This was her explanation to her religious friends. I thank God for the skill which enables me to help others.

I was extremely happy with a letter I received from the mother of a charming young girl who had been having treatment at my clinic. This girl had come to me when she was unfortunately stricken with an incurable cancer. I started treatment and had prescribed some Dr Vogel herbal remedies together with Germanium—the mineral which is also found in the water of Lourdes. She showed slow but steady improvement and I quote from the mother's letter, which I received not so long ago:

My daughter and I have just returned home from Switzerland. We had a marvellous trip to a beautiful country. The holiday had been arranged for children who have either suffered or are suffering from cancer or are terminally ill, to give them the opportunity of meeting their favourite celebrities. In our case my daughter went to a pop festival, as she has been a fan of Duran Duran for the past two years.

It was fantastic that something like this could have been arranged. Physically and mentally she has suffered so much and in the process has seen many who had become friends of hers, die. Some of them in great pain.

This trip has been of tremendous help to her and we both cried with joy because she was so happy. We very much enjoyed the scenery, which was breathtaking and perhaps if you look at the enclosed photograph, you can see for yourself how well my daughter looks at the moment.

Thank you for all your help and advice because, looking at our daughter, we realise that we are seeing a miracle, as she was terminally ill two years ago.

The parents had indeed been informed that the girl's chances were nil and yet today she enjoys good health.

The miracle in this instance is that nature has supplied her with the resources to make her well again. Dietary measures were taken and herbal and mineral therapies were used to which she responded so well.

Sometimes people do not give themselves the opportunity to experience healing. We see too often that once people are following a certain line of treatment and if results are not forthcoming immediately, they become discouraged and discontinue the treatment. Always remember that where there is a will, there is a way. The more positive of mind we are, the better the chances are for a cure.

This maxim was very apt for my approach to the treatment of a patient who could not maintain her enthusiasm till the goal was reached.

It concerned a patient with a chronic back problem. Although very co-operative and full of good intentions, she often considered giving up. I told her that we had to work at it together and often quoted St Augustine to her, who said: "Without God we cannot—without us, God will not." She often used to say to me that it was a miracle that she was still walking. Despite the considerable medical knowledge she had herself, it sometimes took quite a bit of persuasion to keep her going.

However, I was delighted to receive a letter from her surgeon who wrote that the attention she was receiving for her treatment was the very best possible for her condition. Although he was sympathetic towards her problem, he felt that no surgical approach was possible. He stated that the benefit she had received under our care could not be enhanced by any other treatment.

This letter in itself was good therapy for her, because it confirmed what she had been hesitant to admit to herself. The unexpected had happened and for this she will always be grateful. That was all the stimulation she needed to continue.

I have already mentioned the tremendous power of love, which can do so much good and manifest itself in the healing process. Love was the major factor in the treatment of a lady who was full of bitterness and hatred because her daughter had married a coloured man. Her grief and hatred was now directed towards the whole of the coloured races and was so fierce that it had badly affected her personality. She had turned into a bitter and twisted person.

The Bible gives us a very straight verdict on anger and says that it causes the bones to rot (Proverbs 14: 30). This should obviously not be taken literally, but in this particular case, it had indeed affected her bone structure. We went thoroughly into her problems in an effort to reason this out and hopefully to remove this hatred about her daughter's relationship. We talked about love and how love is one of the major commandments in the New Testament. We talked about how miracles can be wrought out of love, as Christ's miracles were done out of love. I pointed out to her that she had lost her daughter because of her prejudice and how she could still repair the relationship before it went beyond the point of no return.

At first she felt unable to co-operate, but finally she

capitulated and changed her attitude. It has not happened overnight but now she is the best of friends with her son-in-law. Along with the improved relationship with her family, her health benefited as well. As the healing process in her mind took place, so did it affect her physical condition. This could be termed a miracle of love.

A pleasant elderly lady was similarly affected. Due to certain circumstances she had become dependent on alcohol and now could not exist without it. I felt very sympathetic towards her, because I knew deep down that she hated the thought of her dependency and of having lost her grip. I pointed out to her how great the energy is within us and how much can be achieved by drawing on this energy. Through it, wounds may be healed or physical problems in our body may be solved, if only we learn how to control our own energies.

She started with simple methods to try and balance this energy, which had gone out of harmony. Eventually the damage she had done to herself was repaired and she was able to fully partake of life again. In a letter to me she wrote: "I am so grateful to you for all your kindness and patience. Above all I thank God for His mercy. After long, self-inflicted suffering I am now a completely new being. Thank you for your belief in me and your encouragement in teaching me about my own energies."

It is not that we necessarily expect *big* miracles to happen. Nature itself is a healing miracle and with some of the apparently simple means given to us in nature, goals may be achieved which will sometimes appear like miracles.

In this context I remember a patient who had suffered from a chronic high blood pressure condition. He told me that a clove of garlic really does contain miraculous healing powers, as was already claimed by previous generations. With the use of garlic he was cured of his high blood pressure, while modern drugs had failed to make any impression. His health problems were now completely under control thanks to this simple natural remedy. Everything which God has given us in nature will react to nature with its great healing powers.

I received a happy letter from a lady who had written to me about her very best friend—a corgi dog—which was sick and in danger of dying. After I had recommended some natural remedies for her dog, she wrote to tell me that a miraculous improvement had occurred: her little friend was completely cured and seemed once more to be enjoying life.

She also wrote that many of her friends and acquaintances had noticed the difference in the dog's condition and were very impressed with what had happened. This case was rather special insofar as the dog was already quite old, but had received a new lease of life.

And then there was the young baby, only five weeks old, whose parents had been told that their baby had only approximately six hours to live. The baby suffered from a serious blood disorder. It was wonderful to see how well this baby reacted to the homoeopathic treatment, much to the astonishment of the doctors. The baby's mother wrote to me afterwards: "I want to express my warmest thanks to you, as our baby is now a healthy lovely boy. Thanks to you and the remedies you prescribed his platelets are now normal. It will be nice when Isaiah 33, verse 24 is fulfilled: "No one who lives in our land will ever again complain of being ill."

It makes our work very satisfying if we see these apparent miracles occur, especially where a helpless baby is concerned, supposedly incurably ill and then we witness total recovery.

A few weeks ago I again saw a gentleman whom I had not seen for quite some years. He was bothered by a rather severe neck problem and after I had checked him over I told him that I was not quite sure what to do. I gently manipulated his neck and gave him some acupuncture treatment, together with some general advice, after which he returned home. During the appointment with his specialist he was told that he needed an operation and had some X-rays taken to confirm that diagnosis.

He then came back to see me and I used some of the therapies described in the chapter on modern miracles. Well, maybe a little miracle took place, because when he went back to the hospital he managed to persuade the specialist to make another X-ray of his neck, as I had advised him.

The specialist came back to tell him that he was baffled by what had happened, but he had changed his mind and did not think an operation was now necessary. He said that the problem which had been there, was almost gone, whereon my patient told him that the pain he had suffered was now much reduced, as the pressure of his cercival disc on the nerve which had caused the agonising pain had been alleviated. He regarded it as a true miracle when I explained to him that the credit should go to a modern adaptation of a very old and tried method. This new therapy has come into its own over the past ten years and serves as an example of how much can be achieved by alternative methods.

Perhaps the best expression of the right attitude to these matters I heard came from a Dutchman who had arrived on crutches. For many years he had been totally dependent on the crutches and, after the successful treatment, when he could throw the crutches away, he said: "Thank you for the excellent treatment. Because of the will to get better, I have also put every effort into your treatment in order to give you, as the practitioner, every possible chance of success. As always with things we cannot understand, we must follow the advice of those who do understand."

If we can pursue the love for others as well as the love for God's creation, we may recall the words of the Russian novelist Dostoyevsky: "Love all God's creation, the whole and every grain of sand in it. Love every leaf, every ray of God's light. Love the animals. Love the plants. Love everything. If you love everything you will perceive the divine mystery in things. Once you perceive it, you will begin to comprehend it better every day and you will come at last to love the whole world with an all-embracing love."

This I am sure is as good a description as we will ever see of the love shown by Christ during His time with us on earth. To those who try to abide by His laws, the above may serve as a guideline.

I know a young person who became totally confused about her religious feelings. She became so worried that it affected her mental health and it had been suggested that she should have a spell in a mental hospital for psychiatric treatment. We talked in depth and she tried to explain what was happening to her and about the different influences which were confusing her so much. She felt as if little devils were causing havoc in her womb and, as I already said, she had deteriorated mentally under the strain. Though she believed in God, she was not able to put her religious beliefs in the right perspective and it was not till she suddenly realised that only the love of Christ could free her from her anxieties and this bewildering confusion, that her condition started to change.

Bit by bit she came to the realisation that she had to accept some of the mysteries of life on which she had pondered. Once she learned to accept unquestioningly the love of God, like a child accepts parental love as a matter of fact, she felt secure and consequently her health returned to normal.

A young man I know also became unbalanced, however not due to religion, but because he felt that he had lost everything worthwhile in his life. He had lost his job and his girlfriend and felt totally isolated. He was considering putting an end to his life, but was meanwhile wondering if he might be possessed.

I told him to think of the body as a large energy field. He should compare the little voices in his head, which worried him so terribly, with a magnetic tape. If we look at a tape we hear nothing as it is an inanimate object. But if we feed the tape into a tape recorder, we can hear what was recorded.

This is also the case with our mind, which works like an electro-magnetic power station. If we are able to balance the energy between mind and body, we can switch off the tape. If we have genuine faith in Him who created us and is always with us, things will fall back into place.

I admit that all this, here on paper, sounds incredibly simple and I know that in reality it is not the case. In the early stages of such problems, however, simple explanations do help to put things in their logical order. If we then pray for guidance it is often heartwarming to see how God's love, once we accept it fully, can guide us back to security and health, and consequently to a fuller life.

Many of my friends will remember old Dr Rowbottom, who recently died at the ripe old age of 95. He was the most active lecturer I have known and has been of great service to many. He knew how to enter into the minds of other people and was able to help and strengthen them psychologically.

Many will remember his story of how he was involved in a serious motor accident. He was more dead than alive when he was brought to the hospital and after examination the doctors declared him dead and his body was taken to the mortuary. While he was lying there an attendant looked at him and wondered, although he was severely injured, if he did not recognise some signs of life. The attendant called the doctors and indeed, although they could hardly believe it, he was still alive.

Dr Rowbottom often told us that in his subconscious mind he did not want to die and he had called on his own energy to keep him alive. He lived for many years after that and was able to help many more people in the unexpected extra years which he had been granted. You will agree with me that what went on in his subconscious mind was inexplicable.

Throughout this book I have been pondering about life and death, cause and effect, and the question "Do miracles exist?"

A number of years ago I remember asking myself that same question. On a Saturday afternoon, when I was not supposed to be working, I arrived at the clinic at the same time as two ladies. One of them was a very well-known person, who looked in extreme pain.

While I opened up the premises she begged me for help. She informed me that she had been to the hospital, because the pain was absolutely unbearable, but there they had told her that they could not find anything wrong with her.

I agreed to have a look at her. I asked her to take a seat and before I had even started with my examination, she passed out. I realised that something was badly wrong. Our principal physiotherapist lived in the clinic and she was fortunately at home. She came immediately when I rang for her and helped me. We took the lady's pulse and after giving her the necessary first-aid, we almost gave up as we could detect absolutely no signs of life. We moistened her lips and tried to revive her with Bach's Rescue Remedy and with Dr Vogel's Cardiaforce, but there was no response. We were waiting for the ambulance we had phoned for to arrive, when out of the blue she opened her eyes. We could hardly believe what had happened.

Through the many years in my line of work I have frequently seen patients faint or seen them in an unconscious state. This, however, was an extremely unusual case, which to this very day is beyond my understanding.

Whenever I see this particular lady I cannot help but think of how strong the life force is and ask myself again the question: "Do miracles exist?" Perhaps, rather than seek an answer to this question, I would suggest that we accept in wonder and amazement the inexplicable.

Again I will leave it to the reader to answer that question according to their own faith and conviction.

There is great comfort to be found in the words of Him who indeed performed wonders and miracles. In the Gospel of John (13: 7) we read how Jesus said to Simon Peter:

> What I do, thou knowest not now, but thou shalt know hereafter.

In a more recent translation it is put as follows:

> You do not understand now what I am doing, but you will understand later.

Bibliography and Literature

Weatherhead, Leslie D., *Psychology, Religion and Healing* (First Edition), Hodder and Stoughton Ltd, London EC4.

Kazuhiko Asai, *Organic Germanium "A Medical Godsend",* Kogakusha Ltd Publishers, Tokyo, Japan.

Allan, L. J., *Painless Pain Control–Body Energy Techniques,* Allan, Margate, Kent CT9 3BT, England.

Sherman, Harold, *"Wonder Healers" of the Philippines,* Psychic Press Ltd, London WC2.

King, Serge, *Kahuna Healing,* Publishing House, 306 West Geneva Road, Wheaton, Illinois, USA.

Westlake, Aubrey T., *The Pattern of Health,* Shambhala Inc., London EC4.

Leck, Sybil, *Diary of a Witch,* Leslie Frewen of London.

Sanchez-Perez, J. M., *Engrammes of the Universe,* Exposition Press, Hicksville, New York.

Ansie Encyclopedia (First Edition 1955), N.V. Amsterdamse Boek en Courant Mij., the Netherlands.

Van Dijk, Paul, *Geneeswijzen in Nederland,* Uitgeverij Ankh Hermes B.V., Deventer, the Netherlands.

Van Nijnatten-Doffegnies, H. J., *Het Geheime Dorp,* Callenbach, Nijkerk, the Netherlands.

Visser, A., *Het Verscholen Dorp,* Wilmace, Dronten, the Netherlands.